ALSO BY KIT AND GEORGE HARRISON

America's Favorite Backyard Wildlife
America's Favorite Backyard Birds

ALSO BY GEORGE HARRISON

George Harrison's Birdwatching Diary
A Beginner's Guide to Bird Watching
The Backyard Bird Watcher
Roger Tory Peterson's Dozen Birding Hot Spots
America's Great Outdoors

The Birds of Winter

The Birds
of Winter

Kit and George Harrison

Line drawings by Michael James Riddet

Random House   New York

Library of Congress Cataloging-in-Publication Data

Harrison, Kit.
The birds of winter / by Kit and George Harrison ;
line drawings by Michael James Riddet.
p.   cm.
Includes bibliographical references
ISBN 0-394-58196-2
1. Birds—North America—Wintering.   2. Bird watching—North
America.   I. Harrison, George H.   II. Title
QL681.H284   1990
598'.0723473—dc20   90-30305

Manufactured in the United States of America

24689753

FIRST EDITION

Book design by Carole Lowenstein

FOREWORD

Anyone who has observed birds in winter has to be impressed with their capacity to survive the fierce elements.

Often we have looked out the windows of our home in southeastern Wisconsin at flocks of dark-eyed juncos, black-capped chickadees, American goldfinches, pine siskins, and cardinals intrepidly clinging to their perches in howling wind and driving snow, trying to sustain themselves in subzero temperatures. We are thankful that we are not out there with them trying to survive.

This respect and concern for the birds of winter is even more weighty on nights when the temperature plunges to $-20°F$ or lower, while fierce winds shake the house and rattle the windows.

We have these feelings even though we know that the birds

In this book, the birds of winter are those species in North America that can spend the cold season north of 40° north latitude.

of winter are well designed to survive winter and, in some cases, even to thrive in the worst of North America's deep freeze. Still, we can't help marveling at the ability of tiny feathered bodies to withstand the most bitter cold.

What is it that allows these birds to stay warm and healthy in a northern winter? How do they differ from their more tropical relatives?

It can be argued that all birds that live in North America from December 22 to March 21 are birds of winter, because some form of winter occurs throughout the entire continent between those dates every year. In Florida, for example, painted buntings are typical winter visitors at feeding stations.

Yet painted buntings are not "winterized" birds. They are not equipped to deal with deep snow and temperatures of −28°F with 45-mph winds—a windchill factor of −96°F. Those were the conditions outside our home on two consecutive January weekends a few years ago. The birds of winter are those that not only survive weather of that severity but handle it routinely.

In our opinion, the true "snowbirds" are those species that winter in significant numbers north of 40° north latitude. That region includes the northern tier of states in the West, Midwest, and Northeast, plus all of Canada and Alaska (see map). We believe birds that can spend the winter north of that line, where the earth and inland waters become frozen solid for an extended period, are the bona fide birds of winter.

Many of the birds of winter are also common backyard species, and we were tempted to feature only those that frequent urban and suburban habitats in winter. But we overcame that temptation because we want to share with you the many spectacular and fascinating winter species that rarely, if ever, are seen in backyards.

This book, then, covers all the species that can winter north of 40° north latitude, except waterfowl and sea birds. Our rationale for omitting waterfowl is that these birds require open water for feeding and roosting, and under normal conditions open water doesn't exist north of 40° north latitide during winter, except in the oceans and other very large bodies of water. There are, of course, water reservoirs and effluent outlets at power plants where thermal energy keeps the water open, and some species of waterfowl may winter there. Canada geese, in particular, have changed their traditions in recent years and are wintering more and more in areas north of 40° north latitude. However, most species of waterfowl fly south well ahead of the freeze. Those that are either sick or injured may not be able to escape the freeze-up of lakes and other water bodies and are likely to perish.

During the past ten years there were two incidents on our little glacier-formed lake in southeastern Wisconsin when ducks became fatally trapped in the ice. One involved a pied-billed grebe, which we watched sadly as the area of open water became smaller and smaller, until the thin ice finally closed in on the doomed bird.

The other incident was even more heartrending. It involved a pair of common goldeneyes. The male was injured or sick and could not leave the lake when it was time to go. The female was reluctant to leave her mate. We saw her fly off the water several times but return a few minutes later to her crippled mate. Meanwhile the area of open water was shrinking by the hour. Finally the open water was so small that even the healthy female could no longer become airborne and she, too, was trapped. The two died that night when the lake locked up. The next morning we watched the crows—nature's clean-up crew—pick at their frozen bodies.

Before describing the intriguing life histories of the birds of winter, we have devoted Chapter 1 to an overview of these hardy birds, their special adaptations, and the distinctive equipment they have for sustaining themselves in winter.

Chapters 2 to 12 present the families and the species of winter birds. They are arranged, for the most part, in the taxonomic order established by the American Ornithologists' Union and published in the sixth edition of the AOU's *Check List of North American Birds*. There are some exceptions to that order: The northern shrike, though a songbird, is also a bird of prey; therefore we placed it with the hawks. And doves and pigeons, though not really chickenlike, seemed to fit well with the gallinaceous birds. The kinglets and waxwings do not belong together, nor do the European starling and the house sparrow, and we've taken some liberties in grouping the horned lark with sparrows and buntings.

Backyard birders may want to check Chapter 13, which contains advice on how to attract many of these very special birds to urban and suburban environments.

Readers interested in photographing birds in winter will find tips in Chapter 14.

If you enjoy taking field trips to see and photograph the birds of winter, you will want to read the Appendix. The list of winter birding hot spots is, as far as we know, the first of its kind ever assembled. It is based on information from more than two hundred parks, refuges, and national forests in the United States and Canada.

ACKNOWLEDGMENTS

Books don't just happen. They require a great deal of time, hard work, and help from many people. The following contributed significantly to the creation of *The Birds of Winter,* and we are deeply grateful:

Dan Johnson, Managing Editor, Random House, our good friend for many years, has also been our book editor. Rare is the book editor who has a personal interest in the nonfiction books he or she is editing. When Dan calls or writes to us, his messages always include something about the birds he and his wife, Hannah, have seen or heard around their home in New Jersey. Dan Johnson played an important role in the concept, production, and final realization of *The Birds of Winter.*

Mada and Hal Harrison, authors of two Peterson Field Guides, *A Field Guide to Birds' Nests* (East and West), published by Houghton Mifflin, and *Wood Warblers' World,* from Simon and Schuster, read our text, offered many suggestions for improving *The Birds of Winter,* and contributed some of the photographs that appear in it.

Richard M. DeGraaf, wildlife biologist for the U.S. Forest Service, Amherst, Massachusetts, coauthor of *Trees, Shrubs and Vines for Attracting Birds,* read the text and helped make it accurate and readable.

Michael James Riddet, wildlife artist, created the superb line drawings, which provide a better understanding of the uniqueness of the birds of winter.

Wildlife photographers Carl, Steve, and David Maslowski, G. Ron Austing, and Leonard and Len Rue helped us illustrate *The Birds of Winter* with their dramatic and exciting photography.

The quality of reproduction of the black-and-white photographs is due in part to the superb darkroom skill of photographer Duane Manthei, who converted many of the black-and-white photographs from color transparencies.

CONTENTS

The Birds of Winter

CHAPTER 1

Designed for Winter

L ike clockwork each autumn, there is a dramatic change
of bird life across North America. Harsh winds and sting-
ing sleet flush out the last of the diehard insect eaters of
summer and usher in the hardy birds of winter.

From their arctic, tundra, and boreal-forest breeding
grounds in the North come flocks of brightly colored invaders,
including yellow evening grosbeaks, strawberry-colored redpolls, purple finches, white-winged and red crossbills, and pine
grosbeaks, along with the feisty pine siskins and American tree
sparrows and the more sedate dark-eyed juncos. Snow buntings rise en masse along rural roads, and stately birds of prey,
including snowy and great gray owls, hunt the fields, marshes,
and woodlands. This is the time of the year when birders hope
to glimpse the three-toed and black-backed woodpeckers.

These very special birds of winter also include some year-round residents that spend the summer months living an easier life on a lush and productive land where food and cover are plentiful, but also are equipped to survive the lean times when food is scarce and the elements are cruel.

Food and Shelter Are Critical

The key to survival for a bird in winter is the same as for every animal that must endure the cold season. It needs to maintain an adequate body temperature by getting enough food each day and by protecting itself against the cold. It also must remain alert to avoid becoming food for another animal that is also trying to keep warm.

The normal body temperatures of birds vary but generally run higher than those of humans. A sparrow's normal daytime temperature, for example, is about 109°F. To maintain that

When food is scarce in the northern forests, millions of birds, like this pine siskin, irrupt southward in search of food.

temperature every minute of the day and have enough energy remaining to keep its furnace going through the night, a sparrow must find a great deal of food every day. Small birds like chickadees and finches eat almost constantly and digest their food rapidly. A chickadee living in temperatures well below freezing must spend about twenty times as much time feeding each day as it does during warm weather, according to *The Birder's Handbook* (Ehrlich et al.).

Not only is sufficient food critical, but the kind of food a bird eats is important. Birds must eat richer food in winter to boost their metabolism. Woodpeckers, which are primarily insect eaters, will adapt their winter diets to include beef suet and seeds when available at feeding stations.

When food supplies are inadequate, birds are forced to migrate to locations where food is available. "Irruptive migrations," those that occur irregularly when food supplies on the breeding grounds are not adequate to carry the birds through winter, are common among birds of prey as well as among the seed eaters. The snowy owl is a prime example of an irruptive migrator. In winters when lemming and mouse populations are low, or when the snowy owl population is too high to be supported by the prey population, the owls head south. Rough-legged hawks, northern goshawks, and short-eared owls are also known for their periodic irruptions.

Redpolls and pine siskins are also irruptive migrators. In some winters they are scarce or entirely absent from feeding stations in the United States. In other years they swarm south by the millions, well into the United States, in search of substitutes for their natural diets of birch and alder catkins. They find some of it in sunflower and niger seeds at feeders. All of these irruptive movements by northern bird species are greeted with great enthusiasm by bird watchers, who revel in the sightings of these hungry vagabonds.

Effect of the Feeding-Station Factor

A surprising number of people who maintain bird-feeding stations in winter are under the misconception that once they start feeding birds they must continue providing food throughout the winter or the birds will starve. We have heard of ded-

American goldfinches and white-breasted nuthatches are among the birds of winter that supplement their natural diets with feeding-station foods.

icated backyard birders who are afraid to leave their northern homes for winter vacations for fear their birds will die.

These people must be reminded that birds have survived for eons without our help, and would survive quite nicely today if there weren't any feeders for them. When we leave home, the birds using our feeders either move to a neighbor's feeders or glean all of their daily food from the wild.

In other words, feeding-station food is supplemental to the birds' natural food supply.

A study of the winter feeding habitats of black-capped chickadees at the University of Wisconsin–Madison, conducted recently by Margaret Clark Brittingham, showed that the birds obtained 20 to 25 percent of their daily energy requirement from feeders, when available, and an additional 75 to 80 percent from natural (wild) food sources.

Brittingham's study also showed that in normal winters chickadees that utilized feeders as a supplemental food source survived at exactly the same rate when the feeding station food was removed as did chickadees that had never been exposed to feeder food.

But Brittingham's research showed that during severe winters black-capped chickadees did benefit from the supplemental food they obtained at feeding stations. The survival rate of her subjects to which sunflower seeds were provided was nearly twice that of birds that obtained all of their food from the wild during severe winters.

The Wisconsin researcher obtained this information over a three-year period by banding 576 chickadees and comparing the survival rates of the 418 that had access to feeder food and the 158 that did not.

Roger Tory Peterson, the dean of bird watchers, whose field guides refined the sport of bird watching, believes that several species of birds have extended their ranges owing to the availability of feeding stations. Northern cardinals, tufted titmice, and red-bellied woodpeckers are examples of species with historic southern ranges that have spread into the Northeast, the Midwest, and Canada. Perhaps the best example of dramatic range expansion due in great part to the availability of feeding-station foods is the spread of the eastern population of the house finch. Released on Long Island some fifty years ago, these birds can now be found as far west as the Great Plains and are due to meet their western kinfolk somewhere east of the Rockies in the next few years.

Flocking with Others

Have you ever noticed that sometimes your feeders are humming with birds and at other times there's not a bird in sight? There may be several reasons for deserted feeding stations: The presence of a hawk is one. Another is that various species of winter songbirds often gather into mixed flocks when foraging for food, and sometimes the flocks are elsewhere. Often, however, when you see a flock of American goldfinches, for example, there will be a band of black-capped chickadees, white-breasted nuthatches, and a downy woodpecker at the feeders, too. The flocking of mixed species is a survival technique in which numbers of birds find more food and enjoy better protection from predators than do individual birds.

Northern cardinals, dark-eyed juncos, American tree sparrows, and many other birds of winter forage together in mixed flocks to find more food and gain better protection against predators.

Caching and Hoarding Are Common

Once an abundance of food is discovered, as at a feeding station, many species of winter birds will eat their fill and then take still more for hoarding. Jays are notorious for caching seeds and nuts. Time and again we've watched blue jays gulp down an astounding number of whole sunflower seeds, lickety-split, one after another, then fly off to stash the loot before returning for more. Though it is debatable whether or not the same bird remembers where it cached the food and returns to eat it, the caches are usually eaten by some needy individual sooner or later.

Nuthatches, for example, are known for stashing sunflower seeds and beef suet in the crevices of tree bark, although brown creepers, chickadees, titmice, and other nuthatches are just as likely to recover the cache.

Woodpeckers have their own methods of caching. Red-headed woodpeckers store acorns, beechnuts, and other seeds in the cracks of dead trees, utility poles, and fence posts within a winter feeding territory which they will defend against other woodpeckers.

The northern shrike, known for its winter diet of small birds and mice, may keep a larder in which it stores excess food by hanging the remains of its victims on the thorns of trees and shrubs or on the barbs of fences.

Hawks and owls are also known for caching the remains of uneaten prey in winter.

Fluffing for Insulation

When the cold becomes a major obstacle to survival, nearly all species of birds fluff their feathers for better insulation against

The keen eyes and ears and skillful hunting tactics of this saw-whet owl and other birds of prey facilitate their survival in winter.

Grouse grow "snowshoes" for walking on snow, but the ring-necked pheasant (tracks shown) is not as well equipped and must wait for a crust to form to negotiate deep snow.

the loss of body heat. This makes a bird appear much larger than when its feathers are laid against its body on a warm day. Tiny muscles in the skin make it possible for the feathers to be raised on cold days in order to trap an insulating layer of air, much as a down quilt does over our own bodies. In addition, most birds have 25 to 30 percent more feathers in their winter plumages than in their summer garbs.

Nor is it unusual for birds to shiver. It is a quick way to turn food into heat, but at a cost, because the birds must then soon find food to turn into more energy or they will die.

The birds also waterproof their feathers several times each day as they preen, using the bill to distribute oil produced by a gland at the base of the tail.

What about the exposed feet and bill? We know that the bill is not skin. It is more like horn and as such is not as vulnerable to freezing. The feet are more sensitive, and we often see a junco or tree sparrow pull one foot at a time up into its breast feathers to warm it.

The feet of many birds are heated with what is called a countercurrent heat-exchange system, in which the arteries run right alongside the veins in the bird's feet and legs. The cold returning venous blood is warmed by the arterial blood, reducing heat loss.

Long Nights, Short Days

Finding enough food to sustain a bird through the short winter day isn't enough. There is the long winter night to be endured as well. In the northern United States and southern Canada, a winter day averages only nine hours of daylight, compared with fifteen hours of darkness, during which most birds do not feed.

Seed eaters, such as finches and grosbeaks, as well as pheasants and grouse, have a special device for dealing with this problem: a well-developed crop in the esophagus into which they pack seeds just before dark. After they have gone to sleep, the seeds are slowly digested throughout the night as energy is required.

Still another adaptation for survival takes over at night. Some birds, perhaps most of those that survive the coldest nights of winter, slow their metabolism, lower their body temperatures, and reduce their heartbeats to conserve energy. Researches have found that some big birds, like red-tailed hawks, as well as tiny birds, like chickadees, become torpid or put themselves into a state of hypothermia on very cold nights in order to conserve enough energy to get started the next day.

Unlike humans, who cannot tolerate a variance in body temperature of more than a few degrees, birds can withstand a fairly wide range of body temperatures. The dropping of their body temperatures at night may have a very positive effect on getting them through the night alive.

Snuggling Helps

How and where they roost is also important for the birds of winter. Some, like partridges and bobwhites, form tight outward-facing circles in which they touch each other, thereby reducing the loss of body heat. Other birds snuggle together in tree cavities or holes in rocks. An extraordinary photograph in the *National Geographic Magazine* a few years ago showed thirteen male eastern bluebirds huddled together in a bluebird box to keep warm. A Russian study of goldcrests, close relatives of the kinglets of North America, revealed that when three of the wee birds snuggled together, each reduced its loss of body heat by 38 percent.

Obviously, the roosting site has to afford some protection from predators as well as from chill and precipitation. Many birds roost in the same kinds of habitat as those in which they nest. Birds that nest in brushy thickets, such as blue jays and cardinals, will usually roost in that kind of cover in winter. Others, like woodpeckers, owls, and chickadees, which nest in cavities, also roost in cavities.

Ruffed grouse take advantage of the protective cover and insulation found in snow. They frequently dive right into six or eight inches of snow to roost for the night or to find shelter from a driving storm. The same is true of snow buntings, which will stay under snow for days until a storm or bitter cold has passed.

Bergmann's Rule

There is still another factor that helps the birds of winter stay warm in cold regions. Birds and other animals living in cold climates tend to be larger than the same species living in warm climates. The cardinals and blue jays in Michigan backyards are quite a bit larger, for example, than those in Florida. Bergmann, a German zoologist, found in 1847 that larger warm-

Despite all of their winter adaptations and energy-saving behavior, the fact that any birds live through winter north of 40° north latitude is an amazing story of survival.

blooded animals living in the colder north are able to produce and conserve heat more efficiently than the smaller members of the same species living in the warmer south, and this survival factor is therefore known as Bergmann's Rule.

Despite all of these special winter adaptations and energy-saving systems and behavior, a great many birds do not survive winter. In fact, more than 80 percent of all young birds are not alive to celebrate their first birthdays. Most die before they are a month old, but a significant number survive the summer only to become victims of predation, starvation, and exposure to winter's cold. The fact that any of them live through winters north of 40° north latitude is an amazing story of survival.

CHAPTER 2

Hawks and Shrike

BALD EAGLE

NORTHERN HARRIER

SHARP-SHINNED HAWK

COOPER'S HAWK

NORTHERN GOSHAWK

RED-TAILED HAWK

ROUGH-LEGGED HAWK

GOLDEN EAGLE

AMERICAN KESTREL

GYRFALCON

NORTHERN SHRIKE

I t was as though a bomb had exploded in the middle of the bird-feeding station. In panic, every bird on the feeders, on the ground, and in the trees above the feeders literally threw itself into the air to escape, a few colliding with the large glass windows of our house in their pell-mell flight to safety. A junco that struck the window lay stunned on the snow. The ambush had worked. The junco would be the victim.

A male American kestrel (sparrow hawk) had skillfully launched this surprise attack by swooping into the patio feeder area for the sole purpose of panicking the songbirds, which were quietly eating. This tactic had worked for him before. The stunned junco would be easy prey.

Gliding down from its perch above the patio, the kestrel pounced on the dazed junco, sinking its talons into the soft

Adult bald eagles, like this one, gather at winter feeding areas near open water, where they feed on fish and carrion.

feathers and thin skin of the helpless gray bird in its grasp. Death was immediate.

With the bird tightly locked in its talons, the little falcon carried the junco up into the basswood tree and then casually plucked a few of the snowbird's feathers with its hooked beak before it began to eat.

Cruel? Perhaps in human terms it appears cruel, but in nature's terms it was just another meal for a bird of prey. Dark-eyed juncos are plentiful in our backyard in winter, as they are in many yards. In fact, they are the most common visitors to feeders in North America, according to the Cornell Laboratory of Ornithology's Project FeederWatch. Juncos are frequent prey for American kestrels, which, like all birds of prey, are

Hawks
and
Shrike

important to the ecological balance of wildlife populations in our yard and throughout the world.

American kestrels are falcons, a subgroup of the hawk family. Other hawk subgroups include the eagles, harriers, accipiters, and buteos. Each subgroup is well represented among the hardy birds of winter in North America, as they all have special equipment that enables them to survive in winter's worst weather.

First-year bald eagles are brownish black. They do not attain pure white heads and tails until their fifth year.

Sharp Tools, Sharp Senses

Hawks are diurnal (daytime) birds of prey. They grasp their food with strong feet that are equipped with sharp, curved tal-

The visual ability of hawks is legendary—thus the term "hawk-eyed." This sharp-shinned hawk, for example, can probably distinguish objects three times farther away than humans can.

ons. Once they have seized their prey, most, like the kestrel, will pluck it or tear it apart with their strong, hooked beaks. A few hawks, including buteos, may swallow small prey whole, without plucking it, and later cough up pellets containing indigestible matter such as fur, feathers, and bones.

The visual ability of hawks is legendary—thus the term "hawk-eyed." There is evidence that hawks can see objects three times farther away than humans can. Part of the reason for their keen sight is that their eyes are larger in proportion to their heads than those of other animals, including man. The large eyes move very little within their sockets. Instead, the bird directs its vision by moving its head, which it can rotate about 180 degrees. Though they employ both binocular and monocular vision, their binocular vision, which allows them to estimate positions of ever-moving prey, is the more effective hunting tool.

Their hearing is also acute, but we do not know as much about the hearing ability of hawks as we do of owls.

Skillful Strategies for Food Gathering

In winter, hawks utilize a variety of strategies to find food and keep warm. Bald eagles come together in winter in fraternal assemblages composed of all ages and both sexes. These large flocks, sometimes numbering in the hundreds, gather at winter feeding areas. Some of the sites are along the northern reaches

All hawks, including this rough-legged, are equipped with strong, hooked beaks for plucking and tearing apart their prey.

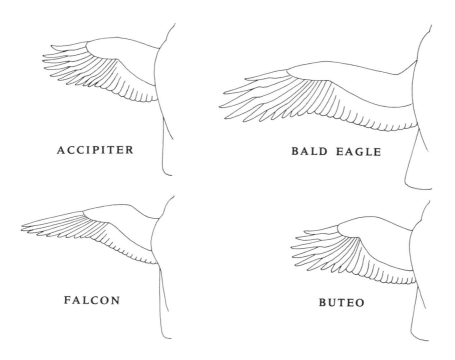

ACCIPITER

BALD EAGLE

FALCON

BUTEO

The shape of the wings of each hawk subfamily facilitates its specialized method of hunting.

of the Mississippi River in Wisconsin, Iowa, and Minnesota, where the warm water discharge from power plants keeps the river from freezing. Eagles find it easy to pick off fish that have been stunned after passing through the power plants' turbines.

Northern harriers, formerly called marsh hawks, hunt by harrying (thus the name). Beating close to the ground on elongated wings, they quarter the prairies and meadows, tirelessly searching for prey. When a target is sighted, the bird stops quickly, hovers, and then drops swiftly to seize its prey.

Accipiters, like the northern goshawk, sharp-shinned hawk, and Cooper's hawk, have shorter, rounded wings, designed for rapid wingbeats as well as gliding. They procure their food in winter by sitting quietly concealed in a tree awaiting an opportunity to ambush their prey. When a quarry is sighted, these swift birds reach top speed with a few quick wingbeats; then they fold their wings and streak in silence to the kill. On impact, sharp talons pierce vital organs as the prey is seized. Northern goshawks usually take their catch to what is called a

Once prey is sighted, buteos, like this red-tailed hawk, glide in to capture their target in their sharp, hooked talons.

butcher's block, where they pluck and skin their food before consuming it. The area around a butcher block may be strewn with feathers, bones, and other remains.

Buteos, such as the golden eagle, red-tailed hawk, and

rough-legged hawk, have broader wings for prolonged soaring, catching rising thermals to gain height. They find food either by soaring over open fields or by sitting in an exposed position, usually at the top of an old tree or on a fence post at the edge of a field, watching for likely prey. Once a victim is spotted, the buteo takes off with vigorous wingbeats, then glides to the target, snatching it from the ground with its talons.

Falcons, like the American kestrel and gyrfalcon, are the fastest-flying hawks. Their long, pointed wings and long, relatively narrow, squared-off tails give them the ability to dive, or "stoop," at speeds of more than 200 mph in the case of the peregrine falcon.

From a lofty perch, which is often a telephone pole, the smallest North American falcon, the American kestrel, scans the countryside in search of food. Ready to hunt, it strikes out, its long, pointed wings beating powerfully as it veers one way

American kestrels (sparrow hawks) are falcons, a subgroup of the hawk family well represented among the hardy birds of winter.

The northern shrike is not a raptor, but it is a bird of prey among songbirds.

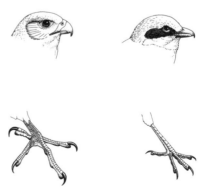

Though shrikes (right) are songbirds, they are birds of prey, with beaks and feet strikingly similar to those of falcons (left).

and then another. Suddenly, the bird faces the wind and hovers, body tilted upward, wings beating lightly. When prey is sighted—perhaps a field mouse—the hawk drops to the ground. Up it comes quickly, back to its watchtower on the pole. Alighting, it dips its long tail, abruptly folds its wings, and starts to tear at its prey.

The gyrfalcon, largest of all falcons, may hunt from a much greater height, at times soaring a thousand feet or higher in its search for prey. But more often it acts like the B-2 stealth bomber, streaking in from only twenty to thirty feet above the ground, hugging the earth's contour in a surprise attack.

The Bird of Prey Songbird

Though the northern shrike is not considered a raptor, it preys on songbirds. Like a hawk, it has a hooked bill for tearing its prey, and strong feet equipped with sharp, talonlike toenails. Otherwise, the northern shrike looks and behaves much like other songbirds. Yet the other songbirds with which it mingles recognize it as a predator. Many times we have seen the birds at our feeding station panic as they do when a hawk approaches, only to find that a northern shrike has landed in the trees above the patio.

Shrikes are also called butcher birds for their habit of impaling insects, small birds, and mammals upon thorns, barbed wire, and twigs for later consumption. In winter they hunt from favorite lookouts from which they can dart out to seize a bird or small mammal. After they have consumed their prey, shrikes disgorge indigestible parts of their food in the form of pellets, or castings, just as raptors do.

THE HAWKS OF WINTER

Bald Eagle—The adult bald eagle is a 35- to 40-inch dark brown raptor with a striking white head, neck, and tail and a wingspan of up to 7½ feet. Its eyes, legs, and bill are bright yellow. First-year birds are brownish black. Their heads and tails do not become pure white until the birds are in their fifth year. The call of the bald eagle is a high and clear *kleek-kik-ik-ik-ik* or *cak-cak-cak.* Though there are southern populations, which remain year-round on their breeding grounds as far south as Florida, northern populations winter in flocks in the northern tiers of the United States near water where they can fish and find carrion.

Northern Harrier—Unlike most hawks, males and females of the 17- to 24-inch northern harrier are different in coloration: Males are gray; the larger females are brown. Both have white rump patches, slim bodies, long tails, and 38- to 48-inch wingspans. Both call a shrill *kee-kee-kee*. In their winter habitat along coasts and marshes from southern Canada to northern South America, they hunt rodents and other small mammals, reptiles, and amphibians, but occasionally take carrion.

The northern harrier (marsh hawk) hunts rodents and other small mammals by "harrying"—beating its wings close to the ground.

Sharp-shinned Hawk—This 10- to 14-inch accipiter with a 20- to 28-inch wingspan is bluish gray above and barred rufous (reddish) and white below. The smaller size and the squared (not rounded) tail of the sharpshin are the most reliable field marks to distinguish it from the Cooper's hawk. Sexes are alike in coloration, but the female is larger. Immature birds are brown and quite streaked. The sharpshin's call is a plaintive *kek, kek, kek.* In its winter habitat of large, remote woods from southern Canada through the United States, the sharp-shinned hawk captures small to medium-size birds, mice, and shrews.

The Cooper's hawk procures its food in winter by sitting quietly concealed in a tree waiting to ambush its prey.

Cooper's Hawk—Like the sharp-shinned hawk, the Cooper's hawk is bluish gray above and barred reddish brown and white below. This accipiter is 14 to 20 inches long with a 29- to 37-inch wingspan. The best field mark, which separates it from the sharp-shinned, apart from its greater size, is its rounded tail. Immature birds are brown, heavily streaked. The call of the Cooper's hawk is a piercing *cuk-cuk-cuk-cuk*. In its winter habitat of deciduous and coniferous woodlands over much of the United States and southern Canada, it preys on birds and small mammals and has an undeserved reputation as a "chicken hawk."

Northern Goshawk—North America's largest accipiter, this 21- to 26-inch beauty with a 40- to 46-inch wingspan is pale gray below and blue gray above, with a black crown and a white streak over the eye. The tail is rounded. The sexes look alike. The northern goshawk's call is similar to that of the Cooper's hawk: *kak, kak, kak, kak,* or *keep, keep, keep, keep.* In its winter forest habitat from Alaska and Canada south into the northern United States, the northern goshawk preys on grouse, pheasants, ducks, gray squirrels, cottontail rabbits, and snowshoe hares.

Red-tailed Hawk—This 22-inch buteo has large, broad wings spanning 50 inches, and a round, fan-shaped tail. The upper side of the tail is rufous and the underside is lighter red and unbarred in adults. Underparts are whitish with dark streaks on the belly and flanks. The immature redtail has a dark gray tail which may be banded. Sexes look alike, except that the female is larger. Their familiar call is a complaining *keeeeeeerrrr.* In their winter habitat of mixed open fields dotted with wood-lots, from southern Canada southward, the redtail preys on mice, squirrels, rabbits, prairie dogs, muskrats, and birds, including waterfowl and upland game birds.

Rough-legged Hawk—A 22-inch buteo with a 50-inch wing-span, the rough-legged is found in two color phases. In the light phase it has a black belly and white tail with a black band at the end. Sometimes the belly is light with a mottled black band. In the dark phase, the black body contrasts with a great deal of white in the flight feathers. It is usually silent in winter. A hawk of open country from southern Canada through most of the United States, the rough-legged often hovers like a kestrel while hunting for mice, lemmings, pocket gophers, and an occasional small songbird.

Golden Eagle—The adult golden eagle is a 30- to 40-inch dark brown bird with a 7- to 8-foot wingspan. In favorable light, the golden brown head and back of the neck may be seen. Unlike the bald eagle's, its legs are feathered to the toes. The brown immature bald eagle might be confused with the golden eagle, but their ranges overlap only occasionally during migration. They are generally silent in winter. Mainly a western species, golden eagles hunt almost exclusively for rabbits and other small mammals on their winter range from southern Canada to the southwestern United States.

The golden eagle, like all buteos, has broad wings for soaring at high altitudes, catching rising thermals to gain height.

American Kestrel—Not much larger than a robin, the male and female of this 10-inch falcon are colored differently. The male has blue-gray wings, while the slightly larger female's wings are brownish red; both sexes have rufous backs and a characteristic black-and-white face pattern. Their call is a shrill *killy, killy, killy, killy.* They prey on songbirds and mice throughout their winter habitat along borders of woodlands, open fields, and pastures throughout the United States and southern Canada.

Gyrfalcon—The largest falcon, the 25-inch gyrfalcon has a 50- to 64-inch wingspan and is found in dark, gray, and white phases. In the white phase, it might be mistaken for a snowy owl, but the long pointed wings and its characteristic falcon flight are distinctive. Its call is a loud, harsh *hyek-hyek-hyek* or *kyek-kyek-kyek.* In its winter habitat of arctic marshes and open country (rarely south into the United States), it preys mostly on ptarmigan, but sometimes takes hares or waterfowl.

The gyrfalcon, largest of all falcons, may sometimes soar as high as a thousand feet in its search for prey.

Northern Shrike—A chunky 10-inch songbird, the northern shrike is big-headed and long-tailed, light gray above and white with gray below, and has a black mask across the eyes. The bill has a hooked upper mandible. The shrike's flight is a series of alternate flappings and sailings low to the ground with an upward sweep to a higher perch at the end as it comes to rest. Its call is a harsh and unmusical *shek-shek*. In its winter habitat of open fields, thickets, and occasionally backyards across southern Canada and the northern United States, the northern shrike preys on small songbirds, mice, and lemmings.

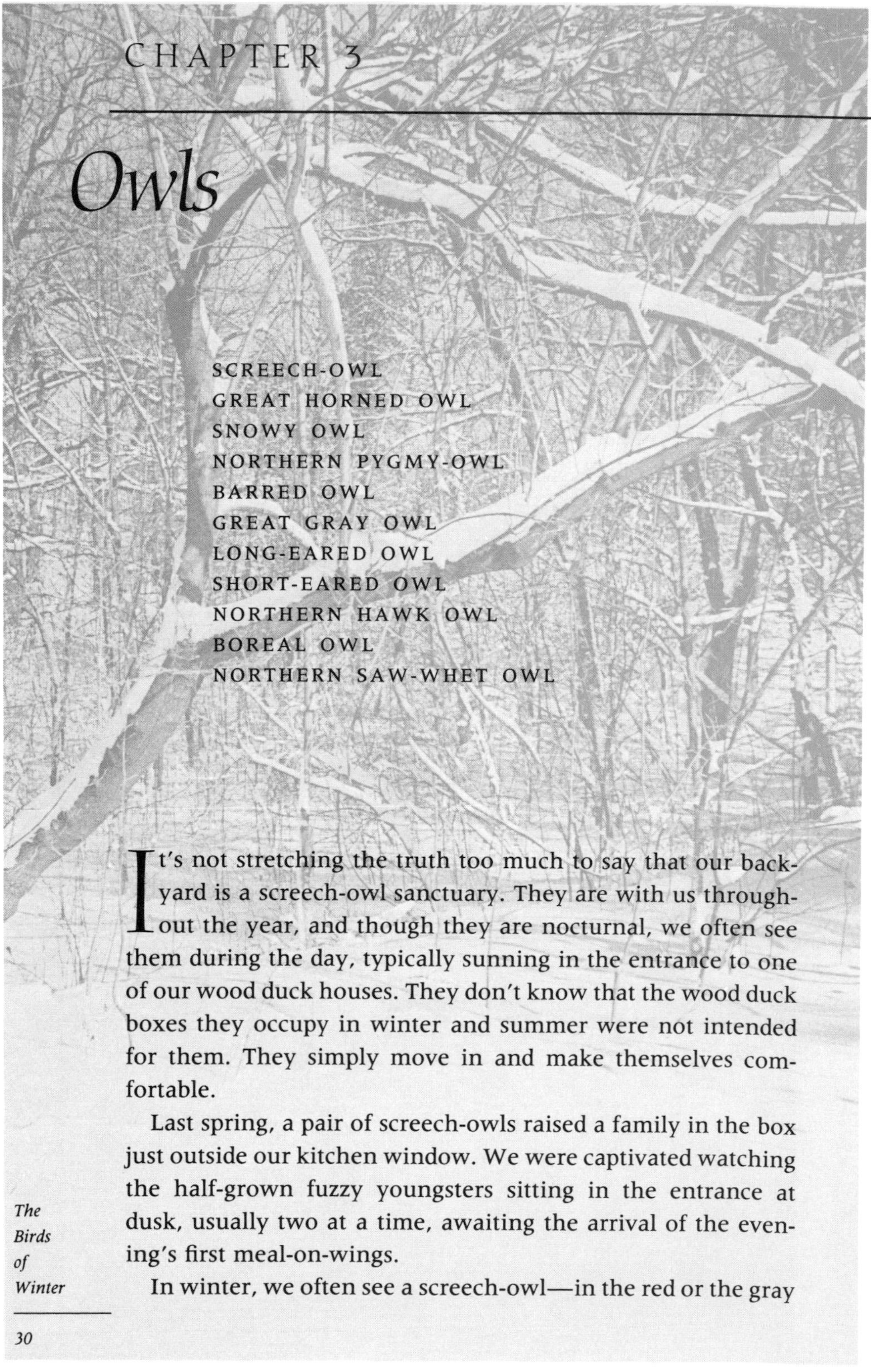

CHAPTER 3

Owls

SCREECH-OWL
GREAT HORNED OWL
SNOWY OWL
NORTHERN PYGMY-OWL
BARRED OWL
GREAT GRAY OWL
LONG-EARED OWL
SHORT-EARED OWL
NORTHERN HAWK OWL
BOREAL OWL
NORTHERN SAW-WHET OWL

It's not stretching the truth too much to say that our back-yard is a screech-owl sanctuary. They are with us through-out the year, and though they are nocturnal, we often see them during the day, typically sunning in the entrance to one of our wood duck houses. They don't know that the wood duck boxes they occupy in winter and summer were not intended for them. They simply move in and make themselves com-fortable.

Last spring, a pair of screech-owls raised a family in the box just outside our kitchen window. We were captivated watching the half-grown fuzzy youngsters sitting in the entrance at dusk, usually two at a time, awaiting the arrival of the even-ing's first meal-on-wings.

In winter, we often see a screech-owl—in the red or the gray phase—roosting in one of the duck boxes, which face south. The owl moves from the interior of the house to the entrance just before dusk, sitting half in, half out, with eyes half open, half closed, seeming to pretend that it doesn't see the songbirds at feeders a few yards away.

But we know that it is very interested in what is happening at the feeders, because each spring when we clean out the houses in preparation for the arrival of wood ducks, we find a variety of songbird feathers inside—red, blue, and yellow feathers, proof that the sleepy occupants of the wood duck houses weren't as innocent as they appeared.

Screech-owls also use the ponds. We have seen them drinking and bathing in the illumination of the patio lights. The most memorable sighting was on New Year's Eve at the very stroke of midnight, when a gray-phase screech-owl started the new year with a bath.

Screech-owls are common backyard birds, though many people are unaware of their presence because of the birds' nocturnal habits.

At dusk, this screech-owl moved to the entrance of the wood duck house to sun itself, eyes half open, half closed.

The feathered tufts on this long-eared owl are not the bird's ears, only ornaments.

Most owls, in fact, are nocturnal, though there are several exceptions. Most are not migratory; the exceptions are those owls that live in the tundra and depend upon prey, such as lemmings and snowshoe hares, whose populations are cyclic. When there is a food shortage, snowy owls and great gray owls are likely to migrate south into the United States in search of a more dependable food supply.

Special Adaptations Enhance Hunting Proficiency

The screech-owl is the smallest owl with "horns," or tufts, on its head. Many believe that these feather tufts are the bird's ears, but they are only ornaments. The outer openings of the true ears are located at the border of stiffly feathered eye discs. The same is true of the great horned and long-eared owls. Their ears are located on the sides of their heads and are surrounded by special deep, soft feathers, which the birds use to funnel sounds to the ears.

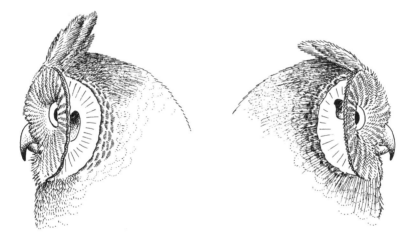

An owl's ears, asymmetrical in both shape and location, are set behind facial disks that gather and funnel sound, enabling the bird to get a fix on its prey.

The ears of an owl are extremely acute, perhaps as keen as any in the animal kingdom. Owls depend greatly on their hearing to catch prey at night, when darkness restricts their ability to see. The facial discs gather and funnel the sound to the ears, like a satellite dish receiving TV signals. To judge distances by hearing, they triangulate the position of the prey with their ear openings, which are not alike either in shape or size, and are not symmetrically located. This creates an asymmetry in the

The eyeballs of this two-foot-long great horned owl are as large as the eyeballs of a six-foot-tall man.

reception of the sound and helps them get a "fix" on their target.

The eyes of owls are also extraordinary. Placed in the front of a large and compressed head, the eyes have full binocular capability and are oversize in relation to the owl's body. The eyeballs of a two-foot-long owl, for example, are as large as the eyeballs of a six-foot-tall man. In addition, an owl can rotate its head 270 degrees to cover an extraordinarily wide field of vision.

Locating its prey with the use of keen sight and hearing, the owl attacks on silent wings. The wings are constructed of very special long flight feathers with softly fringed leading edges that allow the owl to approach its prey very closely without being detected.

Owls, like hawks, have deeply hooked bills and razor-sharp talons to immobilize prey or kill it immediately.

Owls usually carry their food back to a feeding perch to consume it. If the prey is small enough, the owl will swallow it whole and later regurgitate a pellet containing the indigestible fur or feathers and bones. Pellets found under a perch are evidence of an owl's diet.

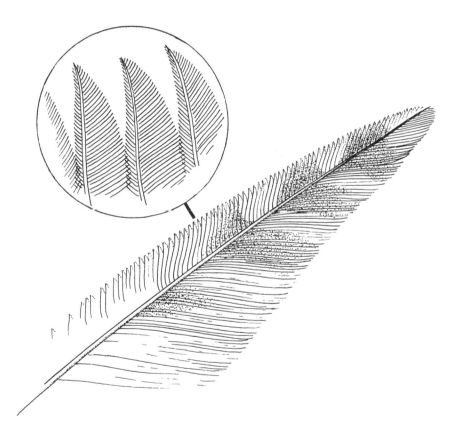

The softly fringed leading edges on an owl's flight feathers allow the bird to approach its prey very closely without being detected.

Roosting-Site Preferences Vary

After feeding, the owl is likely to retire to its roost, often in a tree cavity.

In the case of the screech-owls in our yard, the wood duck boxes, which face south, are a good substitute for a natural cavity. "Screech-owls will readily use a variety of nest boxes for roosting and nesting and have even been found in purple martin houses and untended rural mail boxes. Presumably, a nest box represents simply another form of tree cavity," according to researchers Dwight G. Smith, Arnold Devine, and Ray Gilbert (*Birding,* August 1987). Noncavity roost sites were rarely observed in winter, and most of the cavities and nest-box openings (76 percent) faced southerly, they found.

In winters when lemmings and hares are scarce in the tundra, snowy owls irrupt south into the United States.

In Utah, Nevada, and Arizona, Smith observed western screech-owls roosting in abandoned railroad cars, stovepipes, chimneys, and holes in cacti, and among the beams of abandoned houses, sheds, and barns.

The northern saw-whet owl, smallest of the eastern owls, will also use a tree cavity in which to roost but more often will be found hidden in the dense cover of a tree, such as a hemlock, not far from the ground. A roosting saw-whet appears to be very tame, because it is difficult to disturb it from its roosting perch. "Exceedingly tame—often allowing itself to be picked from a tree and held without a struggle," writes Kim R. Eckert in the *Audubon Society Master Guide to Birding*. But, researcher Ann B. Swengel explains, "this is a survival strategy—not tameness or curiosity on the part of the owl—since there is greater risk of detection and predation if the owl moves than if it remains hidden" (*Passenger Pigeon*, Fall 1987).

When a roosting saw-whet is discovered by songbirds, they usually "mob" the resting owl but rarely drive it away. Great horned owls are also mobbed by other birds, most often by jays and crows, which are sometimes successful in driving the resting bird from its evergreen tree roost.

Snowy owls, those ghost-white birds of the tundra which invade the United States when the food on their home ranges is scarce, roost on the ground or on fence posts in some very busy areas. One of the most unexpected places to see roosting snowy owls in winter is at Logan International Airport, Boston. Apparently they are attracted to the eighteen-hundred-acre field by the tundralike winter habitat and an abundant food supply in the form of mice and rats, which populate the grasslands between the runways and Boston Harbor.

"The owls go about their lives at the airport much as they would in the barren expanses of their home in Greenland and northern Canada," says Norman Smith of the Massachusetts Audubon Society, who banded thirty-six of the owls at Logan a couple of years ago. But the airport isn't always a safe place for snowy owls, which often sit on the white lines of the runway to blend in. Each year a couple of them are hit by planes. However, the danger they create for airplanes is more than offset by the fact that their presence on the field keeps flocks of other birds (blackbirds and pigeons) away from the runways.

Great gray owls also gather in significant numbers in the United States when their food supplies in the north are scarce. Making the journey southward, however, does not assure survival. Roxanna Sayre (*Audubon*, January 1980) told of an invasion of great grays during the winter of 1979. "By April at least 335 gray owls, inhabitants of the remote boreal forests of western Canada, had been recorded in New England, New York, southern Ontario and Quebec—the biggest invasion since 1890–91. Hunger drew them from their normal wintering grounds, but even so eleven owls died of starvation before they could reach food sources—nine in Quebec and two in New England. A twelfth bird was discovered in New York, still alive but too weak to fly.''

In another concentration of 407 great gray owls in southern Ontario during the winter of 1983–84, the birds were so hungry that they took handouts from birders who brought them fresh mice. "That season in the Ottawa area, pet shops sold a lot of mice to birders and photographers who fed them to hungry owls,'' according to Robert Nero (*Birder's World,* September/October 1988). "Some birds were so used to being fed that when a car pulled up, the owls would approach it and wait expectantly. In some instances owls even learned to pluck mice from the hands of excited owl feeders,'' he said.

When food is abundant, owls and other birds of prey may hoard some of it for later consumption. A few winters ago we found a freshly killed, half-eaten gray squirrel cached in an oak woodlot near our home. It was the work of either a hawk or an owl that, having had enough to eat, was saving the rest for later. The cache had not yet frozen, even though the ambient temperature was near zero, but it raised the question of how an owl or hawk can eat food after it freezes.

Frozen Food Gets Thawed

An explanation is offered by William G. George and Robert Sulski. "Sulski put [a great horned owl] into an outdoor cage during a freezing spell in late November, 1976, and by chance left a package of frozen beef cubes in the cage overnight,'' they reported in the *Canadian Journal of Zoology* (February 1984). "The next morning when he approached the cage, the owl was crouched upon the package, its central plumage fluffed up and fanned out to the side; disturbed, it flew to a perch, uncovering a section of meat which obviously was thawing and out of which, just as obviously, a good number of bites had been taken,'' they related. After the owl was released, the researchers continued to keep tabs on the owl. One time, they provided three frozen white lab rats for the owl, placing them in the

The diurnal short-eared owl waits patiently for the sight of prey.

woods where the bird had taken up residence. "It thawed and ate them all," they noted. In another instance, a frozen carcass of a red fox lay in the woods. In December, "the owl was found upon it, thawing its flank."

Both boreal and saw-whet owls have also been observed thawing food in winter.

THE OWLS OF WINTER

Screech-Owl—The 9-inch screech-owl, the smallest owl with "horns," or ear tufts, occurs in two species, eastern and western. The eastern has two color phases, red and gray; the western is gray. Sexes are similar. Screech-owls do not screech. They emit a descending tremulous cry, an eerie, ghostly sound that carries well through the still night. Screech-owls prey on small birds and mice, which they swallow whole. Their typical winter habitat is small woodlots, old orchards, and residential areas from southern Canada south through most of the United States.

Great Horned Owl—The only large owl with ear tufts, or "horns," the 24-inch great horned has a wingspread of over 4 feet. It is mottled brown above and light below with fine barring. Sexes are alike in coloration. The great horned is a "five or six hooter" owl. On its winter woodland habitat, from wilderness to city parks throughout North America, the great horned will prey on a wide variety of birds and mammals. Many wildlife biologists consider it the ultimate predator.

Snowy Owl—The 20- to 25-inch male snowy owl is almost pure white; the larger female's white plumage is flecked with dusky bars. Its calls consist of a deep ravenlike croak and a shrill whistle. In its winter habitat of snow-covered tundra, fields, or marshes in the north (occasionally into the United States), snowy owls prey on lemmings, hares, and ground squirrels.

Northern Pygmy-Owl—This tiny, earless, grayish 7-inch owl has a long tail and white-edged black spots on its nape. It is a species that lives in the coniferous forests and wooded canyons of the West, from Canada south to Mexico; it eats small mammals.

Barred Owl—The large, gray 18- to 22-inch barred owl is almost the size of the great horned owl. The large, round, puffy head lacks ear tufts. Sexes are alike in coloration. The underparts are barred crosswise on the breast, and streaked lengthwise on the belly. Unlike most owls, whose eyes are yellow, the barred's eyes are brown. The barred owl is an "eight hooter," producing two groups of four syllables with the next to last hoot emphasized. In its deep forest winter habitat east of the Rockies from southern Canada south to the Gulf of Mexico, the barred owl hunts mice, squirrels, small owls, and songbirds.

Great Gray Owl—Largest of the North American owls, the 24- to 33-inch great gray resembles its close relative the barred owl

The barred owl is an "eight hooter," with the next to the last hoot emphasized.

in its rounded head without ear tufts. But it is larger and grayer and has yellow eyes, not brown. It is dusky gray in color, with its underparts striped lengthwise. It has a noticeable black chin spot, or "bow tie." The sexes look alike. Its call is like that of the screech-owl, a quavering *whoo-oo-oo-oo,* repeated at intervals. The great gray preys on small mammals, and sometimes small birds, in its winter habitat, the dense coniferous forests of western Canada and Alaska, the northern tier of western states, and occasionally the Northeast.

Long-eared Owl—The size of a crow, the 13- to 16-inch long-eared owl has "ears" (tufts) situated close together toward the center of the forehead. In flight, the tufts are pressed flat against the head. Both sexes are generally dark, with lengthwise streaks underneath. The facial disc is reddish brown, bordered with black. The long-eared owl's winter call is a soft twitter given on the roost before dawn. It preys on mice in its winter habitat of woodlands, thickets, and coniferous groves across southern Canada southward to Florida and Mexico.

In flight, the long-eared owl's tufts are pressed flat against the bird's head.

Short-eared Owl—The harrier of the owl family, the 13- to 17-inch short-eared is a streaked, buffy brown owl. The short "ears" are truly short—only under very favorable circumstances can the feathered tufts be seen. It hunts in the manner of a marsh hawk, during daylight, flying low over fields and prairies, dropping suddenly to the ground to seize its rodent prey. Wintering from southern Canada south into the northern tiers of the United States, it is seldom heard at this time of year.

Northern Hawk Owl—As its name suggests, the 15- to 18-inch northern hawk owl is hawklike in appearance, with a long slender tail. It has a rounded head without tufts, a gray-brown back, and barred breast and abdomen. Facial discs are bordered with black. Legs are feathered to the toes. Its call in winter is a sharp and rapid *ki-ki-ki-ki*. This diurnal hunter forages for rodents and for ptarmigans and other birds in its winter habitat of coniferous forests in southern Canada, north to Alaska, but rarely south into the lower United States.

Boreal Owl—The brown, 10-inch (robin-size) boreal owl is distinguished by its prominent black facial frame and a thickly spotted forehead. Sexes are alike in appearance. Its call is a high-pitched bell-like sound repeated over and over. It is found in the boreal forests of Canada but invades the northern tier of states when its diet of small rodents and birds is scarce.

Northern Saw-whet Owl—Smallest of the eastern owls, the 7- to 8-inch saw-whet is considerably smaller than a screech-owl. Its upper parts are brown, spotted with white. The head is streaked with white and lacks ear tufts. The white underparts

Noted for their apparent tameness, northern saw-whet owls, smallest of the eastern owls, often roost in dense evergreens.

Owls

are striped with rich brown. The facial disc is gray and the eyes yellow. Sexes look alike. The saw-whet is named for one of its many calls, which sounds like the monotonous ringing of a saw being sharpened. To some people, the sound is like a back-up beeper on heavy equipment. Also included in the bird's repertoire of utterances, however, are a variety of whistles, squawks, and notes like the ringing of a bell. It feeds on mice, insects, and small birds in its dense forest habitat from Alaska and Canada to the Southwest and Northeast.

CHAPTER 4

Gallinaceous Birds, Pigeons, and Doves

GRAY PARTRIDGE
CHUKAR
RING-NECKED PHEASANT
SPRUCE GROUSE
BLUE GROUSE
PTARMIGANS
RUFFED GROUSE
SAGE GROUSE
GREATER PRAIRIE CHICKEN
SHARP-TAILED GROUSE
WILD TURKEY
NORTHERN BOBWHITE
ROCK DOVE
MOURNING DOVE

The only way we could peek out of the tiny, frigid blind we shared with Jerry Wunz, Pennsylvania Game Commission turkey biologist, was through a slit just large enough for camera lenses and eyes.

Shortly after daylight we heard the first *perk, perk, perk* of a hen turkey in the brush to the left and then saw her enter the trap zone in front of the blind. A few seconds later, more turkeys arrived, then more, and soon there were at least twenty, all within a few feet of us, all eating the corn bait and murmuring quietly among themselves. With a little luck, these birds would be captured and translocated to another part of the state—or to another state—where there had been no truly wild turkeys for decades.

Jerry had a smile on his face and a finger on the trigger of

Gallinaceous Birds, Pigeons, and Doves

Two truly wild turkeys take the corn bait as a cannon net trap explodes a few feet in front of them.

This Pennsylvania wild turkey played an important role in restoring its species in North America.

the cannon net. The plan was for us to shoot photos at the same time the net was fired, but not before, for fear that we would flush the turkeys.

Bang! The impact of the cannon trap's detonation was jolting. We fired photographs as the cannons fired the net over the flock of birds. We had our pictures and Jerry had his turkeys.

That was twenty-five years ago, and it was an important event in the history of wild turkey restoration in North America. Farm-raised "wild" turkeys had not been the answer. Lacking the hardiness and experience of wild-bred birds to survive the rigors of a northern winter, most farm-raised wild turkeys perished during their first winter afield. Wildlife biologists had come to realize that the only way to bring back viable wild turkey populations was to trap and transfer birds from the few truly wild flocks that remained.

Like other members of the grouse family, the sharp-tailed grouse is well equipped to cope with winter weather.

Wild turkeys, like pheasants, grouse, quail, and doves, are terrestrial birds with stocky bodies and short, stout bills. In winter, when they gather in small flocks, they sustain themselves on a diet composed entirely of vegetable matter.

Turkeys and the ruffed, blue, and spruce grouse are woodland birds and are especially well outfitted to survive northern winters. Prairie grouse, quails, and doves are birds of the open field and can survive the worst of winters if satisfactory shelter is available. Unfortunately for these birds of the farmlands, modern agricultural technology enables farmers to plant crops on every available foot of soil, leaving little or no habitat for wildlife.

Foreigners Not As Hardy

The gray partridge, chukar, and ring-necked pheasant, introduced to North America from Europe and Asia, are not so well equipped to endure the extremes of winter weather in the northern regions of North America. Their winter food is almost entirely grain, and when it is buried by a deep snow, the birds are in trouble.

Ring-necked pheasants will survive severe winter weather as long as they have adequate shelter.

Cold alone is not really a problem for ring-necked pheasants because they can survive temperatures as low as −50°F, according to the Canadian Wildlife Service, if adequate shelter is available. A cattail marsh is ideal for roosting pheasants. They can almost bury themselves in the deep, insulating snow, and the masses of broken cattail stalks provide a windbreak. Pheasants may also leave the ground to roost in dense clumps of spruce trees, out of reach of ground-dwelling predators. Shelter belts—barriers of trees and shrubs planted by farmers as windbreaks—provide safe havens, too, as long as they are at least two hundred feet wide, to exclude the driving snow of blizzards. Blizzards, notorious in the Dakotas, can annihilate pheasants unless they have well-protected roosts.

For most of the winter of 1978–79, for example, there was a heavy snow cover and blizzard conditions in Illinois, according to Dave Ambrose of the Illinois Department of Conservation. When forceful winds drove snow under the pheasants' plumage, soaking the feathers and depriving them of their insulating properties, the birds died of exposure. Others caught in the open suffocated when blowing snow plugged their mouths and nostrils.

According to the South Dakota Department of Game, Fish, and Parks, blizzards have the potential of being the most ruthless killers of pheasants. A three-day blizzard that raged in South Dakota during March of 1966 killed up to 86 percent of the pheasants in several counties.

Fortunately, such devastating blizzards have not struck the entire pheasant range in one winter.

Grouse—Winter Wonders

Members of the grouse family—grouse, ptarmigans, and prairie chickens—are chickenlike birds with short, curved, strong bills. They make relatively brief flights on short, rounded wings. Grouse are well suited for surviving harsh winter weather and actually fare best in snowy winters. For example, snow doesn't hamper their travel, because the grouse grow "showshoes" in fall or early winter, allowing them to graze and browse easily on top of the snow. The ptarmigans' snowshoes are dense mats of stiff feathers that grow on the toes.

Gallinaceous Birds, Pigeons, and Doves

The male ruffed grouse often drums and displays, even in winter, by raising its neck ruff and tail fan.

Other grouse produce horny comblike growths on the sides of their toes that double the foot area.

They often find sufficient protective cover among the trees in which they feed on buds, twigs, and seeds. Many are also adept at snow roosting—plunging deep into snow to escape a predator and to find shelter from severe weather.

When a grouse roosts under two feet of snow, its body heat boosts the temperature of the chamber to as much as 60 degrees higher than that of the air outside, according to biologist John Madson. He also tells of watching a hawk chase a ruffed grouse, which eluded its pursuer by diving into a handy snowbank. Madson reached into the snow, pulled out the grouse, and released it. He did this repeatedly, but the frightened grouse always pitched itself back under the snow.

Ptarmigans—white-tailed, rock, and willow—are the only birds to don white plumage in winter. Other special ptarmigan

Grouse grow "snowshoes" for winter, allowing them to graze and browse easily on top of the snow. In most grouse (left), horny comblike growths on the sides of their toes double the foot area. In ptarmigans (right), the snowshoes are dense mats of stiff feathers that grow on the toes.

When a grouse roosts under snow, its body heat may boost the temperature of the chamber to as much as 60 degrees higher than that of the outside air.

adaptations common to all three are feathered toes that facilitate walking in loose snow, and feathered eyelids and nostrils to keep out snow and for additional protection against extreme cold. The rock and willow ptarmigans are true arctic birds that spend the entire year in the upper reaches of North America. Only the white-tailed ventures south of the Canada–United States border.

At night, each bobwhite in a covey will explode in a different direction from the roosting circle if threatened.

Specialized Winter Strategies

Wild turkeys, too, have the right stuff for winter. Their strong legs with large feet and long toes make superb rakes for scratching up snow and dead leaves in their search for the acorns, nuts, seeds, and fruits that they need for fuel.

Bobwhites are New World quail, small chickenlike birds which keep warm at night by assembling into groups called coveys. The covey of ten to fifteen birds is arranged in a tight circle on the ground, each bird facing outward, and each bird primed at all times to flush in a different direction should danger surprise the flock.

Pigeons and doves are not really gallinaceous (chickenlike) birds. They are plump birds with short necks, small heads, and short bills that are ideal for pecking at seeds, which account for 98 percent of their diet. Strong fliers, they can evade predators on the wing. The fact that they are gregarious and are often found in large flocks in winter is undoubtedly a survival tactic to facilitate finding food and cover and to avoid predation.

Mourning doves frequent feeding stations that offer cracked corn and niger seed.

GALLINACEOUS BIRDS OF WINTER

Gray Partridge—Between a ruffed grouse and a bobwhite in size, the 13-inch gray partridge is a plump bird with a short ruddy tail. It is marked with a dark spot on the belly and chestnut bars on the flanks. The female is paler. Their call is a horse *kee-ah*. At night, they huddle in a circle for warmth and protection against predators. Introduced from Europe, and formerly called the Hungarian partridge, the gray partridge has done well in the hay fields and grain fields of southern Canada and northwestern and midwestern United States.

Chukar—This 14-inch-long Asian game bird is brownish gray above with boldly barred black-and-white flanks, white throat outlined in black, and red bill and legs. Sexes look alike. Its call is a series of loud *chuck-chuck-chuck* notes. In winter, coveys of up to several dozen birds feed on seeds, grain, grass, and weeds in the West.

An Asian import, the chukar spends its winter nights in coveys of up to several dozen birds.

Ring-necked Pheasant—The 35-inch-long male ringneck is iridescent bronze overall, mixed with hues of purple, green, and white. He usually has a conspicuous white neck ring and sports ear tufts on his head, bright red flesh around the eyes, and a long, barred tail. His mate is mottled brown. In winter, the pheasant's calls consist of clucks and loud squawks. The ringneck has done well in the northern tiers of states and into the Canadian prairie, living in cultivated fields, where it eats grain. It is the state bird of South Dakota.

Spruce Grouse—The 16-inch-long male spruce grouse is black and gray above and splotched black and white below. The female's upperparts are browner and she is dull white below,

Silent in winter, the spruce grouse is found in remote coniferous forests, where it eats buds and needles.

thickly barred with black. Silent in winter, the spruce grouse is found in fairly remote coniferous forests of Canada south to the northeastern United States, where it lives on buds and needles of spruce, fir, and larch. Because it often appears to have no fear of people, it is called fool hen.

Blue Grouse—The sooty gray plumage of the 20-inch male spruce grouse is accented by a yellow-orange comb of bare skin over the eye. The female is mottled brown. Its calls are low hootings, clucks, and cackles. In winter blue grouse eat the needles, buds, and twigs of conifers in fir forests of Alaska, the Yukon Territory, and the lower forty-eight states to Arizona and New Mexico. Like the spruce grouse, it is also called fool hen because it is seemingly tame.

White-tailed Ptarmigan—The smallest of the ptarmigans, the 13-inch white-tailed is also the only one that reaches the lower forty-eight states, where it is found in the high Rocky Mountains. It is a grayish brown grouselike bird that trades its summer plumage for snow-white feathers when winter nears. In winter, the only parts of the bird that are not white are its black eyes and bill, so the bird is virtually unnoticeable in the white world in which it survives. Its call is a loud *go-back, go-back, go-back.* In winter it is found in open tundra and on high, rocky, barren slopes from Alaska to New Mexico where it can

Gallinaceous Birds, Pigeons, and Doves

The blue grouse, like its close relative the spruce grouse, is called fool hen because it seems to have no fear of people.

find its staple winter diet of alder catkins, and twigs and buds of willow and birch. The rock ptarmigan and willow ptarmigan, close relatives of the white-tailed, live in northern Canada and Alaska. The willow ptarmigan is the state bird of Alaska.

Ruffed Grouse—The reddish brown or grayish brown 16- to 19-inch ruffed grouse is streaked with black and has a broad black band near the tip of its fan-shaped tail. White underparts are streaked with blackish brown; the throat is buffy. Two color phases are recognized: red birds with ruddy tails, and gray birds with gray tails. Ruffs—large tufts of feathers—at the sides of the neck are usually visible only during courtship display. The ruffed grouse's seldom-heard alarm note is a short *quit-quit.* Its favorite winter food is aspen buds, but it also consumes alder catkins and buds of hazel, willow, and beech in its hardwood forest habitat from Labrador to Alaska and south to northern tiers of the United States. It is the Pennsylvania state bird.

Sage Grouse—The largest member of the grouse family, the 28-inch male sage grouse has a gray-brown body with a black belly and spikelike tail feathers. The much smaller female has a shorter tail. Their calls consist of clucks and cackling. In their sagebrush habitat of the West into southern Canada, the birds rely entirely on sagebrush for their winter diet.

Once a common bird of the Great Plains, the greater prairie chicken now exists only in a few remnant flocks.

Greater Prairie Chicken—The 18-inch greater prairie chicken has yellowish brown upperparts spotted with black, and may be distinguished from the sharp-tailed grouse by its short, rounded black tail and its heavily barred underparts. The female's tail is barred. The male produces a distinctive *coo* during spring courtship displays ("booming"), in which he inflates and then forcibly expels the air from the yellow sacs on his neck. In winter, the greater prairie chicken consumes acorns and grain in isolated areas of the Great Plains, where it was once plentiful.

Sharp-tailed Grouse—The 18-inch sharp-tailed grouse is speckled yellowish brown on its upperparts and is whitish below. The head is slightly crested, and the short, pointed tail appears white in flight. When flushed, it may utter a cackling call. On its winter habitat of brushy prairie, the sharptail feeds on grain.

Wild Turkey—The 4-foot wild turkey is a brilliant metallic bronze. Males (and a few females) have a beard protruding from the breast. Males gobble in spring and may also gobble at other times of the year in response to loud noises. Wild turkeys cluck and utter a *putt* alarm call in winter. They eat acorns and other nuts, seeds, and fruit on their winter range of remote woodlands and inaccessible swamps, farm woodlots, and even some suburban areas.

Northern Bobwhite—The 10-inch male bobwhite has a reddish brown back and wings and a short gray tail. A white line over the eye is bordered with jet black. A conspicuous black necklace separates the white throat from the breast and belly, which are white speckled with black. The female is similar, but has no black under her buffy throat, and her eye line is buffy. The call is a clear *bobwhite* whistle. This seed-eating quail is a permanent resident of the South, but can survive winter north of the snow line in the Northeast and Midwest if there is adequate food and cover.

Rock Dove—This classic 12- to 13-inch pigeon, so common in cities around the world, was introduced into North Amer-

The male wild turkey has a "beard" that protrudes from his breast and drags in deep snow.

The bobwhite is a southern bird but can survive northern winters if there is adequate food and cover.

Common in cities, this rock dove (pigeon), a European native, is a pest at North American bird feeders.

ica from the rocky coasts of Europe. It eats grain wherever available and is a frequent visitor to city bird feeders. Its *coo* is familiar throughout North America from southern Canada southward.

Mourning Dove—Both sexes of the 11- to 13-inch mourning dove are fawn brown. In flight, the pointed tail shows white spots and the wings produce a whistling sound. The call is a mournful *coo.* The mourning dove is one of the most common and widespread birds in North America. In winter, mourning doves feed on grain and other seeds in farmlands and suburban areas from the northern tiers of the United States south to the Gulf and into Mexico.

CHAPTER 5

Woodpeckers

RED-HEADED WOODPECKER
RED-BELLIED WOODPECKER
DOWNY WOODPECKER
HAIRY WOODPECKER
THREE-TOED WOODPECKER
BLACK-BACKED WOODPECKER
PILEATED WOODPECKER

Woodpeckers in winter conjure up vivid memories of a day afield in a snowy forest of western Pennsylvania some years ago. The woodland was very quiet, except for the crunching of snow beneath our boots.

We stopped frequently to listen for birds, and after hearing only an occasional black-capped chickadee or tufted titmouse, we moved on. Then, at one listening post, we heard a loud, sharp, single note. *Kik.* It was a bird neither of us had ever heard before.

Easing through the mature oaks and hemlocks toward the call, we heard another *kik,* this time much closer. We slid quietly around the next few trees to the edge of a little clearing under a tall, dead hemlock. Raising our binoculars simultaneously, we zeroed in on a big black woodpecker at the top of

Once or twice every decade or so, the black-backed woodpecker migrates south into the United States in winter in search of wood-boring insects and their larvae.

the dead snag. We were looking at a life lister . . . the first sighting in our lives of a black-backed woodpecker.

We studied the 10-inch black bird, with its distinct yellow cap and black bars on its white sides, for several minutes, watching it flake away large chunks of dead wood with its heavy bill as it searched for insect pupae and larvae. It called *kik* several more times before leaping off the snag and flying deeper into the woods.

From that moment, the black-backed has always been, for us, the epitome of the winter woodpecker. But all woodpeckers are exciting birds because they are so splendidly designed for life in their tree-trunk environment. From the diminutive

7-inch downy to the magnificent 16-inch pileated, all have special adaptations to facilitate making a living in that habitat throughout the year.

The most stalwart of the woodpeckers reside year-round on their breeding grounds, which for many is north of 40° north latitude. Yet that black-backed in Pennsylvania was a long way from its breeding territory in the boreal forests of Canada.

Under normal conditions, it would have remained in Canada through the four seasons, but occasionally the black-backed and its close relative, the three-toed woodpecker, fly south for the winter. This happens only once or twice every decade or so; and when it does, it's probably because there is too much competition for food, resulting from a banner production year for the woodpeckers, or a low production year for their insect prey.

Otherwise, like all the woodpeckers that spend winters north of 40° north latitude, they remain in or close to their home ranges, where food and cover are normally plentiful.

In fact, the winter diets of woodpeckers vary little from their summer diets—wood-boring insects and their pupae and larvae, plus some seeds and nuts.

Foraging Equipment: The Bill and Tongue

When foraging, woodpeckers can utilize their distinctive bills like jackhammers to exert brute force to get at insects in the wood. At other times the heavy bills are used like toothpicks or table forks to gently pry the morsels out.

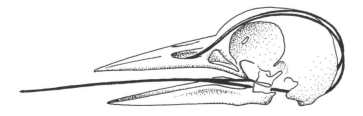

The exceptionally long, sharp, barb-tipped tongue of the woodpecker curves around the back of the skull, where it divides into two horns and is attached in the nostril.

Woodpeckers

People sometimes wonder why woodpeckers don't get concussions—or at the very least, headaches—from their vigorous hammering. Above the sturdy chisel-shaped bill, where the bill meets the skull, is a very thick bone that is more or less honeycombed. With plenty of air spaces, almost spongelike, it serves as padding and absorbs most of the shock of the blow as the bill hits its target at about fifteen miles per hour, sometimes hundreds of times a day. The muscular neck, too, which furnishes the drive for the jackhammer bill, aids in absorbing some of the shock.

The highly specialized tongue is also used to obtain food. It is an exceptionally long, sharp, barb-tipped, wormlike instrument, which can extend out as much as three times the length of the bill. It curves around the back of the skull, where it divides into two horns and is finally attached in the nostril. Equipped with a kind of automatic recoil system, the tongue can spear insects and their pupae and larvae like a harpoon. In addition, the tongue is covered with gluey saliva that can make matters rather sticky for woodpecker prey.

Grasping the Tree

Such remarkable equipment in the woodpecker's head requires a special support system at the other end of the body to give the bird leverage. First are its toes. Unlike most birds, whose feet have three toes in front and one behind, woodpeckers (except the black-backed and three-toed) have two toes in front and two behind, making it possible for them to clamp themselves to the sides of trees.

Their strong, stiff tail serves as a third leg, so that these birds have with them at all times a handy camp stool. With the firm grip of their feet, plus the steadying factor of the tail, these expert climbers are braced securely on their tripod at nearly any angle on a tree. Moving up tree trunks, using the tail as a third leg, they leisurely forage around the entire trunk or branches of a tree before moving on to the next one.

Sometimes they use their feet to hang underneath their food. We watched a pair of upside-down pileated woodpeckers pick wild grapes from a vine in the top of a white oak while we sat eighty feet below them. They behaved exactly like par-

The strong, stiff tail feathers on a woodpecker, as on this downy, are used like a third leg.

rots we have seen in the tropics. Hanging upside down with their heads and tails pointing upward, the birds picked the wild grapes with their bills. They moved from one bunch to another, remaining upside down with their bodies curled into balls.

Pileated woodpeckers have a particular fondness for carpenter ants and will consume hundreds of them after boring into the core of a decayed tree to expose an ant nest. More than twenty-six hundred carpenter ants have been found in the stomach of a single pileated woodpecker.

Woodpeckers

The pileated, the largest woodpecker in North America, is especially fond of carpenter ants, which it often finds in the oblong cavities it chisels.

Cozy Cavities

Finding and consuming sufficient food is just part of the formula for winter survival north of the snow line. Woodpeckers also know how to provide themselves with warmth and cover when required.

At night and during particularly severe weather, woodpeckers stay warm by roosting in cozy tree cavities, which they fashion themselves or adapt from cavities that already exist. A woodland that lacks dead or dying trees in which woodpeckers can chisel cavities will have no resident woodpeckers in either winter or summer.

This was the case in Ohio, where the red-oak borer had badly ravaged a forest, causing loggers to remove all the dead trees, which had provided cavities for woodpeckers. Because

Polystyrene trees were used to attract downy woodpeckers to an Ohio forest infested with the red-oak borer. The birds excavated cavities in the artificial trees. *Woodpeckers*

Traditionally a resident of the Southeast, the red-bellied woodpecker has extended its range to north of the snow line.

downy woodpeckers are such effective exterminators of the red-oak borer, researchers there made special efforts to attract the little black-and-white dynamos back to the infested forest. To accomplish this, they erected a large number of eight-foot-tall polystyrene trees, which would permit the woodpeckers easy drilling. The downies responded, excavating holes for nighttime roosts in over 80 percent of the plastic trees.

To attract downies and other woodpeckers to backyards, in winter or summer, a few standing dead trees are helpful. The natural insect food living in the bark can be supplemented with beef suet at the bird feeder. At night and during storms, the woodpeckers will roost in cavities of the dead trees.

A shortage of roosting cavities doomed a male red-bellied woodpecker, the first to pioneer in our neighborhood in southeastern Wisconsin, a number of years ago. One night in January, soon after his arrival, the temperature dropped to −29°F, and apparently the hapless bird didn't have a suitable cavity in which to roost. We found him the next morning on top of the snow, on his back, feet up, frozen in the clinging position.

Band recoveries show that some woodpeckers have done very well at surviving winter and have, in fact, lived what seem to be exceptionally long lives. One hairy woodpecker nearly reached the age of sixteen, and a red-bellied was recovered at the ripe old age of twenty years, eight months. Most of the longevity records for woodpeckers, however, fall between nine and eleven years.

THE WOODPECKERS OF WINTER

Red-headed Woodpecker—The entire head of both sexes is bright red, the underparts are white, and the back is black. Its call note is *queer, queer, queer.* This 9-inch woodpecker is primarily a bird of the Southeast but has expanded its range north of the snow line into the Northeast and Midwest. It can be found in open deciduous and coniferous forests, farm woodlots, and backyards. Its diet is mostly insects, including ants, wasps, and beetles, plus some corn and fruit. It will also visit backyards for suet placed in tree-trunk feeders, and will take sunflower seeds and cracked corn.

Red-bellied Woodpecker—A more descriptive name for this 9-inch bird would have been "Zebra-backed" woodpecker. Its belly isn't red, though it has a red patch underneath. Males have a bright red crown and nape; females have only a red nape. Both are gray below. Their call note is a rolling *churr-churr-churr* or a cackling *kek-kek-kek.* Traditionally a resident of the southeastern United States, the red-bellied has extended its range north of the snow line in the East and upper Midwest. Found in both coniferous and deciduous forests, as well as in

Woodpeckers

This red-headed woodpecker, like most other woodpeckers, will eat beef suet to supplement its insect diet.

orchards, gardens, and backyards, the red-bellied eats large quantities of destructive insects, as well as acorns, beechnuts, pine seeds, and fruit, and some suet and sunflower seeds from feeders.

Downy Woodpecker—The most common backyard woodpecker, the downy, like the hairy, is named for the feathers that surround the nostrils in its bill. The downy, at 6½ inches, is about 3 inches shorter than its look-alike relative, the hairy. Like the hairy, it is a black-and-white woodpecker, and the males have a red spot on their heads. Its call note is a softer *pik* than that of the hairy and its whinny is higher pitched. Found in backyards across the United States and Canada, the downy likes open forests, mixed growth, orchards, and swamps. Its diet is primarily insect food but occasionally includes some seeds or fruits. It is fond of beef suet at backyard feeding stations and sometimes takes sunflower seeds, cracked walnuts, and peanut butter.

Hairy Woodpecker—Named for the hairlike feathers around its nostrils, the hairy woodpecker is a black-and-white bird with two red spots (looks like one spot) on the back of its head (the female has no red spots). Nine and a half inches long, it is larger than the downy, and its bill is much heavier in proportion to its body size. Its notes are a sharp *peek* and a slurred whinny. A winter resident of the northern United States and southern Canada, the hairy is found in both coniferous and deciduous forests, wooded swamps, and backyards. Its insect diet is supplemented with small amounts of seeds and fruit, as well as feeding-station offerings such as beef suet, sunflower seeds, cracked nuts, and sometimes peanut butter.

The bill of the hairy woodpecker is larger in proportion to its body than that of its close relative, the downy woodpecker.

Three-toed Woodpecker—A heavily barred black-and-white back distinguishes the three-toed from the black-backed woodpecker. Otherwise, the 9-inch bird looks similar to the black-backed, even to the yellow cap on the male. Though it is normally silent, its call note is a *pik.* Like the black-backed, it inhabits coniferous forests in Alaska, across Canada, and south along the Rocky Mountains. During winters when there is a shortage of wood-boring insects and their larvae, on which this bird depends for food, it will migrate southward or to lower altitudes.

Black-backed Woodpecker—The black-backed is black above and white below, with black-barred sides. The 10-inch male has a yellow cap, which the female lacks. Its stout, straight bill is about as long as its head. The call is a sharp, loud *kik.* A resident primarily of Canada, the black-backed also occurs in northern New England and down the Cascade Mountains and the Sierra Nevada. It migrates south into the northern United States when winter food shortages occur on its home range. Found mostly in boreal coniferous forests, it prefers insects which live under the bark in standing dead timber, so it is common in areas that have been burned or where trees are windthrown.

Pileated Woodpecker—The largest woodpecker in North America, the 16-inch, crow-size pileated is a striking black-and-white bird with a fire-red crest which, on the female, does not extend to the bill, as it does on the male. The call note is a rising and falling *wuck-a-wuck-a-wuck-a.* A winter resident of southern Canada and the northern United States, the pileated feeds on insects, especially carpenter ants, by excavating oblong holes in the trunks of standing and fallen timber. At feeding stations, it may be attracted to beef suet.

Corvids

I f men wore feathers and wings, a very few of them would be clever enough to be crows," Henry Ward Beecher once remarked. Among the most intelligent, clever, noisy, and curious birds in the world are the members of the crow family, the Corvidae. They also seem to have a penchant for getting themselves into trouble.

While camping in Algonquin National Park, Ontario, we were welcomed and continually visited by gray jays, sometimes called camp robbers or whisky jacks. The latter name comes from an old Indian name for the birds, "wiss-ka-chon" or "wis-ka-tjon," which was corrupted to "whisky john" and later "whisky jack." But "camp robber" would prove to be far more appropriate in this instance.

Shortly after our arrival we had lunch, sharing some scraps

"Camp robber" is a good name for the gray jay, notorious for its friendly thievery at northern campsites.

with the companionable birds. The gray jays seemed to be particularly fond of the baked beans we offered to them in a pie plate near our picnic table, but they partook of everything that was accessible.

The next day, when we emerged from our tent, the jays were waiting for us, looking for handouts. Never more than a few feet away, they seemed to be our constant escorts, even when we walked short distances from our camp.

Just before dinner on the second day, while washing after a hike, Kit removed a ring from her finger and set it on the table. In a flash, one of the jays swooped in, grabbed the ring in its bill, and flew back to the tree above the table. Alarmed, Kit shouted at the bird, jumped up on the table, and grabbed at the camp robber just as it was about to fly off. Fortunately, the bird dropped the ring when it was frightened off its perch.

Before breaking camp the following day, we found that we

were missing several other, less valuable, items, which we assume had become the booty of the camp robbers—a hair clip, a tiny purse mirror, a ballpoint pen, and a half-eaten roll of Life Savers.

Blue jays and crows act much like gray jays, though they are not as likely to seek out people. When George was a boy helping his dad with bird photography, there often were blue jays and crows living in the Harrison household, waiting to be photographed. In those days it was not illegal to keep them in captivity, and in some respects, it is too bad that young people can't have them as pets today. Much can be learned from keeping wild pets, and corvids are among the best. Many of the world's greatest naturalists had wild animals for pets in their youth.

George remembers that it was not safe to leave anything shiny lying around the house when the birds were on the loose. Invariably, they would pick up these objects and carry them around or stash them where no one could find them.

As it approaches a feeding station, the blue jay sometimes mimics the call of a hawk, frightening the other songbirds from the feeder.

From Soup to Nuts

Corvids are largely omnivorous—they'll eat anything from nuts and seeds to fruit, meat, and carrion. One study identified 650 different items eaten by 2,118 crows collected in 40 states and several Canadian provinces.

Along the coast, especially during the winter months, mollusks contribute an important element in a crow's diet. Crows commonly carry clams, scallops, mussels, or sea urchins to a considerable height, then let them fall on the rocks to be broken, exposing the edible contents. This technique is also employed by other birds, notably herring gulls.

But there is more to the food story than simply what they eat. Corvids are also great hoarders, and that trait alone has saved many a corvid from starving in winter. Some corvids have a throat pouch into which they pack seeds, nuts, and other food for transport to a cache.

In 1961, W. J. Bock discovered glands in the mouths of gray jays that secrete a sticky fluid that coats the food before the jay hides it. This gluey substance makes seeds, insects, and other bits of food hold together in a small wad that will stick to the side of a branch or in a cavity or some other caching spot.

Apparently the corvids can remember where they have cached their food after considerable time has passed. Biologist Victor H. Cahalane once flushed a Clark's nutcracker from the snow-covered ground beneath a Douglas fir. The bird "had dug a hole three or four inches in diameter at the top, at an angle of perhaps 30 degrees, through the hard-packed snow to the sloping ground," he related. "At the bottom of the excavation, frozen to the ground litter, was a Douglas fir cone." Cahalane reported that the snow was eight inches deep, and there was nothing on the surface of the snow to indicate that there was food—a pinecone—underneath. Yet, the bird had done no exploratory probing. With unerring accuracy, the nutcracker had zeroed in precisely on target.

Jay vs. Jay

There is no honor among thieves, they say, and plundering corvids, notorious for pilfering the caches of other corvids, per-

Like other corvids, this Clark's nutcracker has a throat pouch into which it can pack seeds, nuts, and other food for transport to a cache.

Corvids, like this blue jay, seem to remember where they have cached their food, even after considerable time has passed.

sonify that maxim. Steller's jays, for example, have been monitored robbing the newly cached seeds of Clark's nutcrackers just after the nutcrackers left the cache sites, and have also been observed stealing food cached by gray jays. Kristi Burnell and Diana Tomback of the University of Colorado–Denver Department of Biology reported their observations of a Steller's

Corvids

Steller's jays are known to plunder the caches of other jays.

jay stealing food cached by gray jays in Rocky Mountain
National Park. A gray jay would take a piece of bread and fly
into the woods to cache it. "One or two Steller's jays would
follow the gray jay into the woods, and as soon as the gray jay
stashed it, a Steller's jay would fly in and attempt to take the
cache," the researchers reported. In several instances, the gray
jay displaced the Steller's, removed the cache, and flew deeper
into the woods, leaving the Steller's behind. At other times, the

Steller's stole the cache. Once, two Steller's jays teamed up to accomplish their heist. While the first distracted the gray jay, the second made off with the prize. Another time, the gray jay remained nearby for several minutes after securing its cache. But as soon as it left, a Steller's was on the scene. Although the gray tried to oust the thief, the Steller's had already purloined the cache. "These observations suggest that food-cache pirating may be a frequent foraging behavior on the part of Steller's jays," they concluded.

The Clark's nutcracker is named for Captain William Clark of the Lewis and Clark expedition.

Flocking for Survival

Though corvids compete with each other for food in winter, they nevertheless seek one another's company while feeding and roosting. Among crows, winter flocks can swell to huge numbers. Not far from where we live, wintering crows come to roost in the spruce trees of a Milwaukee County golf course each night from October to April. At dusk, commuters on the expressway north and west of the city see long strings of the

Corvids

In winter, American crows congregate in huge roosts numbering thousands of birds, presumably for mutual protection.

birds arriving from all points to spend the night together in the trees. This communal roosting behavior has undoubtedly evolved for mutual protection, based on the fact that there is often safety in numbers.

Unless the large concentrations of birds are far away from people, they are usually regarded as pests, and local governments are called upon to "*do* something!" In one famous incident in the Midwest, 328,000 crows were annihilated in one season when dynamite bombs were placed in the roost during the day and exploded at night. In that case there wasn't much safety in numbers.

Part of the problem with winter flocks of corvids is the ruckus they raise. Corvids are noisy birds; that is their nature.

They do, however, have a vast range of vocal utterances, many of them harsh, some soft and melodious, others imitative. Pet crows have learned to repeat some of the words and phrases of their human keepers and often display an uncanny knack of knowing when to use them. "One crow was taught to pick pockets, and whenever it would encounter an empty

Corvids, including this American crow, are noisy birds with a vast range of vocalizations.

pocket, it would fly off screaming, 'Go to hell!'" according to T. R. Kerth, an Illinois writer.

"Mobbing" is another interesting trait of corvids, particularly the jays. They just can't seem to pass up an opportunity to harass a sleeping owl or resting hawk. Once a target is located, the alarm is given and every jay in the area is called in for the party. If the victim pretends that nothing is happening, the aggressors will eventually tire of the game, but some owls can't take the heat and are driven off their roosts.

THE CORVIDS OF WINTER

Gray Jay—Resembling a huge chickadee, this crestless 12-inch jay is gray with a black hood and white forehead. Its fluffy plumage, most noticeable in winter, exaggerates its size. Its vocalizations include many harsh calls. In its winter habitat of coniferous forests in Canada, Alaska, and the northern tiers of the United States, and south along the Rockies, the gray jay

Corvids

eats anything offered at campsites but has a fondness for meat and fat in winter.

Steller's Jay—The 13-inch Steller's is a crested blue jay of the vast coniferous forest area of western North America. Its fore-parts are black or dark brown; its wings, tail, and underparts are deep blue. Among its many calls are *schaack, schaack, schaack* and *klook, klook, klook.* Steller's jays are found in winter throughout the West, from Alaska to Mexico. They eat nearly anything, but at that time of year their diets are almost entirely composed of tree mast—acorns and other nuts.

Blue Jay—Bright blue above and whitish below, the 12-inch blue jay has a prominent, sassy crest. The blue jay's most com-mon calls are *jay, jay, jay* and *teacup, teacup.* In its habitat of mixed hardwood forests throughout the East, the blue jay eats almost anything but in winter relies mostly on nuts and seeds, including feeding-station offerings of suet and sunflower seed.

Clark's Nutcracker—A black tail and wings, with conspicuous white patches in the wings, distinguish the 12-inch Clark's nutcracker from the gray jay. Its call is a repeated squawking *char-r-r-r.* Named for William Clark of the Lewis and Clark expedition, the nutcracker is found only in the juniper and pine forests of the high West, where it consumes great quan-tities of pinyon pine nuts and whatever else is available. (This bird can be relied upon to be looking for handouts at Rainbow Curve in Rocky Mountain National Park.)

Black-billed Magpie—Graceful in flight, with its long irides-cent tail feathers streaming behind and its white patches flash-ing with every wingbeat, the magpie is a handsome bird. It is large—almost 20 inches long—with the tail making up half the bird's length. Its plumage is iridescent greenish black, with white on the shoulders and abdomen. Among its many unpleasant calls and whistles is the one described as a high *cääk, cääk.* The black-billed magpie eats more insects than other corvids and in winter consumes a great deal of carrion and some small mammals. It is a bird of western canyons and streamsides from Alaska to the Southwest.

Handouts of peanuts at Rainbow Curve in Rocky Mountain National Park never fail to attract Clark's nutcrackers.

RAINBOW CURVE

s 10,829 feet, more than a mile higher than the G
e miles to the east, reaching to the horizon. The
low, Hidden Valley, with the course of Hidden

Corvids

Because short rounded wings restrict its flight, the black-billed magpie must remain close to thick brush, into which it can escape when threatened.

American Crow—Like most other crows and ravens of North America, the 18-inch American crow is all black. Its tail, fan-shaped in flight, and its longer, thinner bill distinguish it from the larger common raven. Its best known call is *caw, caw, caw,* but like all corvids, it has an impressive repertoire of vocalizations. The American crow eats nearly anything, and in winter it often consumes carrion found on highways. It winters in open and wooded country throughout the United States and into southern Canada.

Common Raven—Considerably larger than a crow, the all-black 24-inch common raven has a 4-foot wingspan (that of a crow is less than 3 feet). The bird's croaking notes are entirely different from the crow's cawing, and its voice is the best field mark, when it can be heard. In its varied winter habitat of mountains, coasts, canyons, and deserts throughout the West from Alaska to Mexico, and in southern Canada and the Northeast, the common raven is omnivorous but is largely a scavenger of dead animals and fishes.

Considerably larger than a crow, the common raven has a heavy, arched bill, which is sometimes described as a Roman nose.

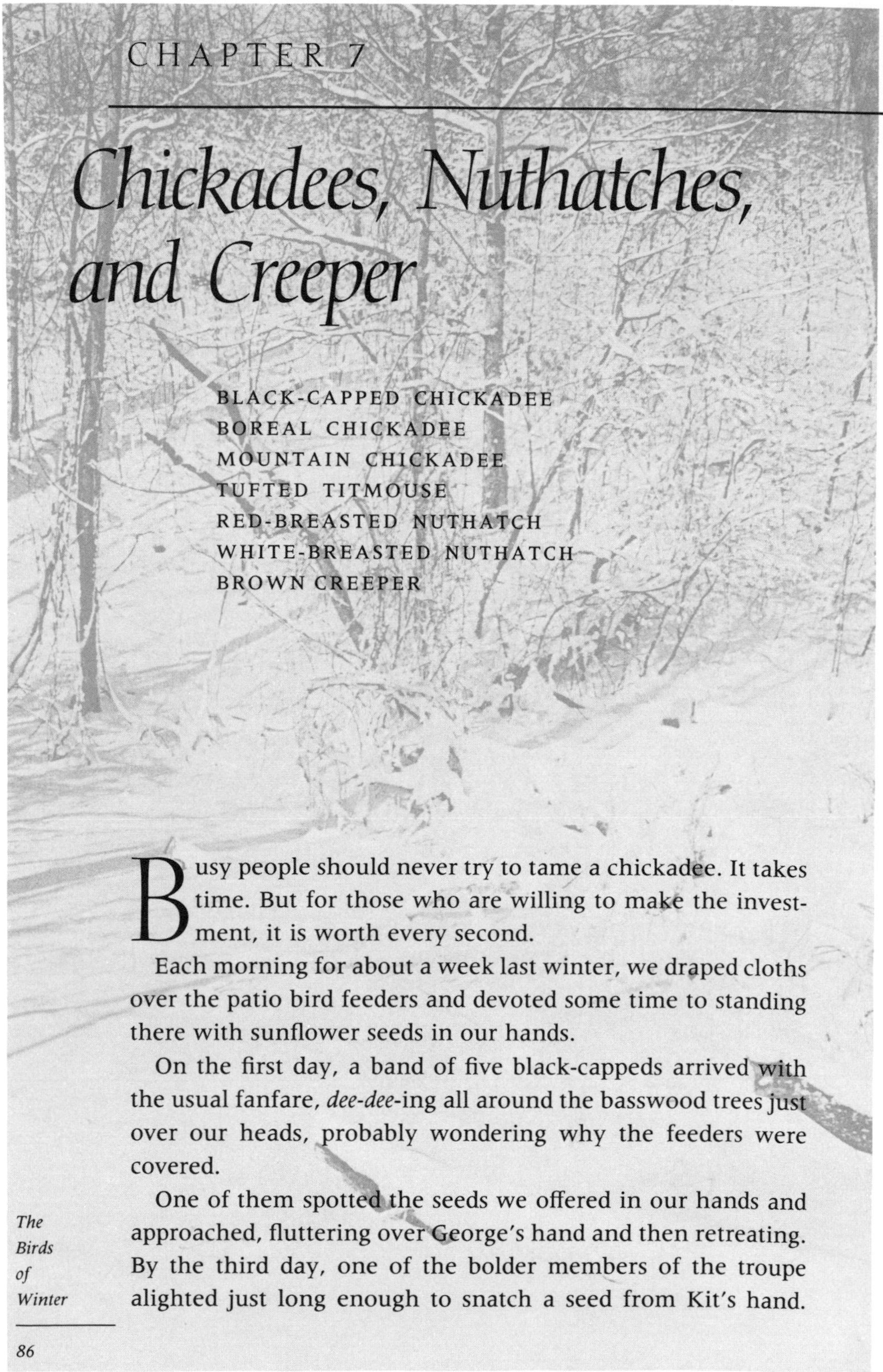

CHAPTER 7

Chickadees, Nuthatches, and Creeper

BLACK-CAPPED CHICKADEE
BOREAL CHICKADEE
MOUNTAIN CHICKADEE
TUFTED TITMOUSE
RED-BREASTED NUTHATCH
WHITE-BREASTED NUTHATCH
BROWN CREEPER

B usy people should never try to tame a chickadee. It takes time. But for those who are willing to make the investment, it is worth every second.

Each morning for about a week last winter, we draped cloths over the patio bird feeders and devoted some time to standing there with sunflower seeds in our hands.

On the first day, a band of five black-cappeds arrived with the usual fanfare, *dee-dee*-ing all around the basswood trees just over our heads, probably wondering why the feeders were covered.

One of them spotted the seeds we offered in our hands and approached, fluttering over George's hand and then retreating. By the third day, one of the bolder members of the troupe alighted just long enough to snatch a seed from Kit's hand.

Coauthor George Harrison enjoys the feel of a black-capped chickadee selecting a sunflower seed on his hat at the Schlitz Audubon Center, Milwaukee, Wisconsin.

Eventually they became so accustomed to us that we didn't need to cover the feeders.

As far as we're concerned, no other species better represents the world of winter birds than these tiny imps. They always seem to be happy and active. No matter how cold or how gloomy the day, or how empty the sunflower seed feeder, they remain in character—cheerful, bouncy, fluffy balls of black, white, and gray feathers which never seem to tire.

It would be an inexcusable ingratitude to write of winter without noting the chickadee, author Bradford Torrey commented (*The Rambler's Lease,* 1889). He described the chickadee as "the most engaging and characteristic enlivener of our winter woods; who revels in snow and ice, and is never lacking in abundant measures of faith and cheerfulness, enough not only for himself, but for any chance wayfarer of our own kind."

They're also very curious. We often experiment with new feeders on our patio, and each time we set one out, there is no doubt as to which bird will be the first to try it. In fact, more often than not, the trusting little chickadees are waiting right there while the new feeder is being installed, cocking their heads and watching intently with beady black eyes, ready to sample the fresh seed.

Black-capped chickadees are very curious. This one is waiting patiently for a new feeder to be filled with seed.

Their responsiveness to patient taming is legendary. Chickadee enthusiast John Woodcock told of one that was so tame it would often swing head downward from the peak of Woodcock's cap, or cling to his lips and peck at his teeth. "If I held my hand out with nothing in it, he would always hop to my thumb, and peck the nail two or three times, then hold his head on one side, and look into my eyes, as if to ask me what I want," he related in a 1913 issue of *Bird Lore.* "I tamed several more chickadees that winter; eight out of twelve, as nearly as we could count, were quite tame," he wrote. "It was rather amusing when I took the .22 rifle to shoot rabbits! After the first shot was fired, I was attended by several chickadees. They made aiming almost impossible, for every time I raised the rifle, one or two birds would perch on the barrel, completely hiding the sights."

Chickadees and titmice, members of the Old World family known as tits (Paridae), are gregarious, but less so than finches and sparrows. Chickadees band together in family groups of five to nine birds, which stay together throughout the winter season until it is time to pair and nest in the spring. They roam the winter woods in search of their natural food, mostly insect eggs and seeds, but will never pass up an opportunity to dine on sunflower seeds at a feeder. If there is not enough natural food to maintain the band throughout winter, they will range farther afield, but they do not exhibit any kind of set migration pattern.

The tufted titmouse, historically a southeastern species, is now also found well north of the snow line.

Supercharged Ball of Feathers

Chickadees and titmice have supercharged energy levels to keep body temperatures up and the potential for predation down. In order to sustain that energy level through a cold winter day, and have enough fuel left over in their metabolic furnaces to survive an even colder night, chickadees have to maintain a high level of food intake—at least twenty times higher than in summer—or run the risk of freezing to death. The same is probably true for the nuthatches and brown creepers that live in the same winter climate.

Winter nights are particularly difficult for these little dynamos. "A few years ago, Susan Chaplin, a Cornell graduate student, conducted studies of the biology of black-capped chickadees to determine just how they were able to survive cold northern winters," recounted Charles R. Smith, acting executive director of the Cornell Laboratory of Ornithology (*Newsletter to Members,* Winter 1979). "In midwinter, when the days are shortest and the weather often is quite cold, chickadees have their greatest need for energy to heat their tiny bodies. At the same time, because of the shorter days, the amount of time available to them for feeding is limited. During the day, black-capped chickadees maintain a body temperature of around 108°F," he reported.

Susan Chaplin found a striking difference between chickadees and other birds, Dr. Smith said. When the body temperatures of black-capped chickadees were measured at night at air temperatures of 32°F, it was found that their body temperatures averaged as much as 20 degrees lower than their normal daytime temperatures. "At such lowered body temperatures, all normal bodily functions, such as breathing and heartbeat, became slower. At such low body temperatures, the rate of heat loss is reduced too, and the demand for energy to replace the loss of heat from the body surface goes down," Dr. Smith explained.

Survival Strategies

The choice of roosting site, another critical element for getting through the winter nights, varies for these birds. Chickadees, titmice, and nuthatches often disappear into the abandoned nesting cavity of a woodpecker, or perhaps into the same cavity in which they were raised a few months earlier. Others roost in dense evergreen groves, which shelter them from wind and snow. Brown creepers apparently cling at night to

Upside down is right side up for this foraging white-breasted nuthatch.

the same tree-bark habitat on which they spend their days. One person reported seeing brown creepers clinging to the rough stucco in the entrance to her front door; another observed them roosting in the opening of a hollow beam at the end of a barn.

The foraging techniques of these birds, which must find a great deal of food each day, also differ. In their search for spider eggs, chickadees investigate every nook and cranny, prying under bark, into cracks, and even under the eaves of our house and balcony. They seem to be hanging upside down as much as they are right side up, a talent that allows them to scour the tree branches, twigs, and bark for the most hidden morsels.

Nuthatches customarily fly to the upper branches of trees and then work their way down the tree trunk head first, checking each scale of bark, each twig and branch, for insect eggs. The nuthatch's technique—moving upside down from top to

Chickadees, Nuthatches, and Creeper

bottom of the tree—is the reverse of other birds' and enables it to detect prey that might be missed by those whose movement is from bottom to top.

The brown creeper, a rather solitary bird among its own kind in winter, often joins bands of chickadees and nuthatches to feed. It forages in still another fashion, following the opposite of the nuthatch's foraging circuit. It flies to the bottom of a large tree and then creeps upward over the bark in a spiral route until it reaches the top, and then flies down to the base of another tree. As it passes over the tree bark, it scrutinizes each crevice, picking up tiny bits of food that it finds hidden in the bark.

Each of these birds has a somewhat different eating style, and when they are at feeders, we can watch their various techniques. A chickadee or titmouse selects a sunflower seed with its sharp little bill, places the seed between and under its dainty black feet, and then hammers the edge of the shell with its bill. After about a half dozen hits with the pointed hammer, the seed usually surrenders its prize.

Nuthatches tackle it differently. After some messy thrashing about in the seed, some of which is scattered on the ground, the nuthatch selects one with its longer and thinner bill, flies

A chickadee places a sunflower seed between and under its feet and then hammers with its bill on the edge of the shell until it surrenders its prize.

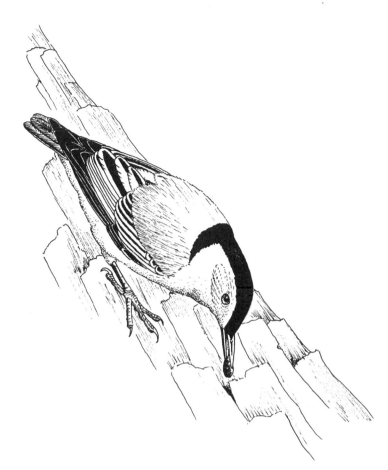

The nuthatch selects one seed, flies with it to a nearby tree, wedges the seed into a crevice in the bark, and then hammers it open with its bill.

with it to a nearby tree, wedges the seed into a crevice in the bark, and then hammers it open with its bill. This procedure gives the bird its name, which is derived from "nut-hack," a reference to its habit of hacking or pecking nuts to open them.

The brown creeper is not as enthusiastic about feeding-station food as are the chickadees and titmice. It will often approach the beef-suet feeder on the tree trunk but spends more time searching the bark around the feeder than eating the suet. We assume that it is more interested in the bits of suet that have been wedged into the bark by suet-eating woodpeckers than in the large chunk of suet itself. Ornithologist John Terres reports that brown creepers will eat a mixture of peanut butter, cornmeal, and suet if it is spread on tree bark.

Nonstop Chatter

Communication among all these birds is important and continuous. As a band of chickadees roves through a woodland, its members chatter nonstop with their characteristic *chick-a-dee-dee-dee* and occasionally the more romantic *fee-bee.* When one member loses sight of the others, there is never a problem catching up; it merely follows the chatter.

Nuthatches also maintain communication. Paired through the winter, they establish and defend a feeding territory of twenty-five to thirty acres. Their nasal call note, *yank, yank, yank,* keeps the pair together as they hunt for food.

The brown creeper's call is so quiet that it is not often heard—and less often recognized. The diminutive bird's call is as mouselike as its demeanor: a faint little *see-ee-ee.*

Constant communication also contributes to the gathering of these species in a kind of movable feast. Though the nuthatch and creeper interlopers are not an integral part of the chickadee or titmouse clique, they are casual associates, and it is not unusual to see them all arrive together at a feeding station.

Nearly invisible in its tree-bark niche, the brown creeper typically searches the bark around the suet feeder rather than eating directly from the feeder.

A bird of the coniferous forests, the red-breasted nuthatch eats conifer seeds but will also frequent backyard feeders.

THE CHICKADEES, NUTHATCHES, AND CREEPER OF WINTER

Black-capped Chickadee—A plump, black-billed 5-inch acrobat, the black-capped chickadee has a distinct black cap and bib, white cheeks, and buffy sides. Sexes look alike. Its *chick-a-dee-dee-dee* chatter is often accompanied by the *fee-bee* song. A year-round resident in southern Canada and the northern tiers of the United States, the black-capped chickadee spends winter and summer in the same habitat, deciduous and coniferous forests and rural woodlands, where it searches for insect eggs and relishes sunflower seeds from feeders where available. The black-capped chickadee is the state bird of both Maine and Massachusetts.

Boreal Chickadee—The 5-inch boreal chickadee is a brownish version of the black-capped, though both have a black bib. Sexes look alike. Its *chick-a-dee* call is less lively and more wheezy than the black-capped's. In its coniferous forest habitat in Canada, it searches for the eggs of spiders and other insects.

Mountain Chickadee—A white eyebrow and pale gray sides distinguish the mountain chickadee from the black-capped, and its *chick-a-dee* call is more hoarse; its *fee-bee* song is a descending whistle. In winter, the mountain chickadee migrates to coniferous forests in lower elevations, where it eats the eggs of spiders and other insects.

Tufted Titmouse—A mouse-gray bird, the 6-inch tufted titmouse has a gray crest and brown flanks. Its *peeto-peeto-peeto* call can often be heard in winter. This pioneering species from the Southeast has extended its range to north of the snow line in the Northeast and Midwest. In winter it depends heavily on acorns and other tree mast, supplemented with insect eggs, and sunflower seeds at feeding stations.

Red-breasted Nuthatch—Like all nuthatches, the little 4-inch red-breasted has short legs, a flat body, and a large head. Its strong, rather long bill is slightly upturned. The red-breasted nuthatch can be distinguished from other nuthatches by its pronounced white eyebrow stripe set off by a black line through the eye, and by the black on top of the head and neck. The crown is black in the male and dark grayish blue in the female. The back, wings, and tail are mostly grayish blue in both sexes. The rusty-colored underparts that give this species its name are paler in the female. The nasal *nyah-nyah-nyah* call of this bird, like a tiny tin trumpet, is higher pitched than that of the white-breasted nuthatch. Though many stay in their coniferous forest habitat in the northern United States and Canada through winter, some fly south, deeper into the northern tiers of the United States. They eat conifer seeds and feeding-station food.

White-breasted Nuthatch—A little bluish gray bird with a white breast and a black cap and nape, the 5-inch white-

Sharp-shinned Hawk

Dark-eyed Junco

Blue Jay

*Evening Grosbeak Pair
at Feeder*

*Black-capped
Chickadee*

TOM PAUGH

*Mourning Dove at
Feeding Station*

Hairy Woodpecker

Purple Finches

American Goldfinches

Red-bellied Woodpecker

Screech Owl

Male Northern Cardinal

Ring-necked Pheasant

Clark's Nutcracker

Downy Woodpecker

breasted nuthatch has tawny flanks and white patches on each side of its tail. Sexes are alike in coloration. It seems to defy the law of gravity by walking down tree trunks head first. Its call is a characteristic *yank, yank, yank.* A year-round resident in the United States north to southern Canada, the white-breasted eats the eggs of spiders and others insects, plus acorns and other tree mast, as well as feeding-station food.

Brown Creeper—A slender 5-inch bird, the brown creeper is brown-streaked above and white below. When it forages for insects in tree bark, the bird is often invisible; it flies like a dry leaf in the wind. Its *seep-seep-seep* call is so thin and weak that it can easily be missed. The brown creeper winters within its breeding range, which extends north into southern Canada.

The brown creeper scours its tree-bark habitat for insects.

CHAPTER 8

Kinglets and Waxwings

GOLDEN-CROWNED KINGLET
RUBY-CROWNED KINGLET
BOHEMIAN WAXWING
CEDAR WAXWING

Taxonomists tell us that kinglets and waxwings are not related and have very little in common. But to watchers of winter birds, the species have some similarities.

When we watch the kinglets and waxwings during early and late winter, the delicately marked birds are generally quiet and well-behaved. They flutter at the ends of branches high in trees when foraging for their natural food. They show no interest in the foods we offer in the bird feeders but frequently visit our pools for drinking and bathing. They winter in small flocks as far north as southern Canada and as far south as the Gulf Coast (except the Bohemian waxwing, which does not journey south of the northern tiers of the United States).

Kinglets Concentrate on Insect Prey

Kinglets are the smallest of winter birds. Despite its size, the golden-crowned is a hearty sprite that spends the winter in much of its summer range. Hardier than its close relative, the ruby-crowned kinglet, it is found much farther north during the winter—as far north as Maine and Nova Scotia.

What is remarkable about kinglets is that their diets are so specialized, consisting almost entirely of animal matter. In winter they scoop out the eggs and larvae of spiders, mites, and other insects found in the woodlands they frequent. Fluttering

Like other birds of winter, this golden-crowned kinglet fluffs its feathers for insulation against the cold.

at the ends of pine and spruce boughs, they examine them thoroughly for insect eggs and larvae.

Ornithologist Edward Forbush spent one Christmas Day watching golden-crowned kinglets hunting their insect food amid the pines in Massachusetts. "Each one would hover for a moment before a tuft of pine needles, and then either alight upon it and feed, or pass on to another," he wrote. Forbush examined the needles after the kinglets had left them, but could find nothing on them. He noted, however, that when a

Kinglets and Waxwings

Kinglets forage for tiny insect eggs and larvae by fluttering at the ends of pine and spruce boughs.

bird was disturbed before it had finished feeding, the spray from which it had been driven was invariably found to be covered with numerous black specks, the eggs of plant lice. "Evidently the birds were cleaning each spray thoroughly," he concluded. Forbush supposed that the trees had been infested with countless thousands of mite eggs, for the insectivorous birds lingered in the area until late March.

Though the ruby-crowned kinglet winters farther south than the golden-crowned, it forages in much the same way, searching carefully at the base of each pine needle and in the pockets between the needles, frequently fluttering in midair in front of the clusters.

A Glutton for Berries

Waxwings flutter, too. If there is a hatch of insects, waxwings can be seen flying out from a tree perch, gobbling an insect on the wing, and then flying back to the same tree to wait for another.

The diet of waxwings changes with the seasons. At the approach of autumn, they switch from insects to fruit and berries, literally gorging themselves at every opportunity. "The appetite of the cedar-bird is of so extraordinary a nature as to prompt it to devour every fruit or berry that comes its way," John James Audubon commented in 1842. Though their favorite is the berry of the European mountain ash, they also relish the berries of cedar trees, for which they are named, and will stuff themselves on crab apple, serviceberry, chokecherry, pyracantha, privet, and mulberry, given the opportunity.

The cedar waxwing's winter diet consists largely of berries, which it devours greedily.

When cedar waxwings attack the mountain ash berries on our terrace, they seem ravenous, always hurrying to get to the next berry. A waxwing will bow down from above to snatch a berry off the branch, often fluttering to maintain its balance. Then it straightens up and usually raises its head as a sword swallower might to let the berry roll into its gullet. It's a treat to watch the waxwings when, as sometimes happens, one flips a berry into the air and catches it on the way down.

Later in the winter, when fruit becomes scarce, waxwings may revert to seeds, but rarely to the seeds offered at bird feeders.

Dainty Voices

The voices of waxwings and kinglets are distinctive, but anyone with even the slightest hearing impairment will find them difficult to hear. The cedar waxwing's high-pitched wheeze or light chain-rattling sound has so little tone quality that it appears to be one of the least developed calls of all songbirds.

The same is true of the Bohemian waxwing's weak voice, which is inaudible except at very close range, or when many birds together produce the sound.

The waxwing's call might be confused with the golden-crowned kinglet's, which is also a short, faint, high-pitched *tsee, tsee, tsee.* It, too, is difficult for many people to hear.

Strangely, the ruby-crowned kinglet's voice is a marked exception. People who hear the tiny ruby-crowned's song for the first time are amazed at its volume. They would be even more astounded to learn that the kinglet's lower larynx, the sound-producing organ, is not much bigger than a pinhead, and that the muscles that control it are almost microscopic. "If the strength of the human voice were in the same proportion to the size of the larynx, we could converse with ease at a distance of a mile or more," Dr. Elliott Coues speculated.

Elegant, Debonair Attire

The most memorable aspect of the waxwings and the kinglets is their sleek and silky, yet conservative, plumages. The subtle grays and browns of the waxwing are accented with red tips

Flocks of hungry cedar waxwings can strip a tree of its fruit in a matter of hours.

on the ends of their secondary wing feathers; these little spots look like bits of sealing wax—thus the name "waxwing." This exquisite plumage also provides superb insulation when fluffed up on a very cold day to trap an extra layer of air space between the bird's body and outer layer of feathers.

Kinglets may be tiny, but their long, thick, fluffy plumages also are excellent insulation against the cold. Combined with

Kinglets and Waxwings

their high activity levels and equally high food intake, their metabolism keeps the kinglets warm and active through the depths of winter.

THE KINGLETS AND WAXWINGS OF WINTER

Golden-crowned Kinglet—The golden-crowned kinglet is a chunky mite, a mere 3½ to 4 inches long, olive green above and grayish beneath, with a conspicuous white-and-black-bordered crown patch. In the male, this patch is orange; in the female, yellow. The golden-crowned has a white stripe over the eye. Their year-round call is a high *tsee, tsee, tsee.* In their habitat of coniferous forests and cedar swamps from southern Canada southward almost to the Gulf of Mexico, their winter diet is nearly 100 percent insect eggs and larvae.

Ruby-crowned Kinglet—The scarlet patch on the 4-inch male's grayish olive crown is usually concealed. It is exposed when the bird is excited and lifts its crown feathers. The crown patch is absent in the female. The ruby-crowned's two white wing bars, its stubby tail, and its nervous fluttering distinguish

The ruby-crowned kinglet's high metabolism keeps the bird warm and active in the depths of winter.

it. Its call is a wrenlike lisping *zhi-dit*. It winters from Oregon to Maryland, foraging for insect eggs and larvae in coniferous forests and swamp woodlands.

Bohemian Waxwing—The 8-inch Bohemian waxwing is a larger edition of the more common and more widely distributed cedar waxwing. It may be distinguished from the cedar waxwing by the white in its wings and the chestnut undertail coverts, which are white in the cedar bird. In addition, the Bohemian lacks the wash of yellow that is evident on the belly of the cedar. Its call is a weak trilling *zir-r-r-r*. It is named Bohemian for its unpredictable winter travels through the coniferous and birch forests in southern Canada and the northwestern tiers of the United States. It eats berries, fruits, and sap.

Cedar Waxwing—This crested brown bird, 6½ to 8 inches long, with a black mask over the eyes and a broad yellow band at the tip of the tail, has red tips on the ends of the secondary wing feathers. Its call is a high-pitched hiss or wheeze. The cedar waxwing eats cedar berries, for which it is named, but also enjoys other fruits and berries, particularly those of the mountain ash, throughout its range from southern Canada to the Gulf of Mexico and Mexico.

CHAPTER 9

The Big Finches

NORTHERN CARDINAL
PINE GROSBEAK
RED CROSSBILL
WHITE-WINGED CROSSBILL
EVENING GROSBEAK

A mong the memorable days we have spent with bird banders over the years, one in particular stands out. We were assisting a master bander with her mist nets in exchange for the opportunity to photograph the birds she captured. For us, the bird of the day was a male cardinal. Our prize, however, turned out to be a surprise as well. We didn't expect the bird to be so vicious and aggressive. Indignant at being a captive, the cardinal clamped its formidable cone-shaped bill on the bander's thumb, inflicting a painful half-inch gash. Though bleeding, our intrepid bander friend perse-vered long enough for us to record a close-up photograph of the cardinal's brilliant red-and-black face with its menacing red bill for the front cover of *National Wildlife* magazine.

A sharp, stout, strong bill, tailor-made for efficient seed-

National
WILDLIFE
AUGUST-SEPTEMBER 1973
DEDICATED TO IMPROVING THE QUALITY OF OUR ENVIRONMENT · PUBLISHED BY THE NATIONAL WILDLIFE FEDERATION

A bird bander's perseverance made this cover photograph of a northern cardinal possible.

cracking, is a common feature of the large winter finches—the cardinals, grosbeaks, and crossbills. It is an essential tool in their acquisition of the tree seeds upon which they depend for their food. Cardinals and grosbeaks are proficient at using these bills to open sunflower seed. The seed is rolled up on edge with the tongue, then snapped in two with a crunch of the heavy mandibles. The shell falls from the bill as the nut meat is eaten.

The Big Finches

Bills designed for cracking seeds. Clockwise from top left: red crossbill, northern cardinal, evening grosbeak, purple finch.

Twisted Bills for Prying

Crossbills, which normally do not visit backyard feeders, rely almost completely on seeds from coniferous trees for their food. To glean seeds from pinecones efficiently, these birds have evolved highly specialized crossed bills. Although this structure, with the upper and lower mandibles twisted and overlapping, makes it more difficult for the birds to pick up seeds from the ground, it is perfect for prying apart pinecone scales to expose the seeds. The crossbill inserts its closed bill into the cone and then forcefully opens it, the action separating the scales that protect and hide the seeds. The food is then removed with the scooplike tongue. When clambering about in the branches of a conifer, the bird uses its bill almost as much as its feet and is not averse to hanging by one foot while reaching out with the other for a better hold.

"During an invasion of white-winged crossbills in a hemlock forest in western Pennsylvania," bird authority Hal H. Harrison recalled, "I stood directly under a hemlock tree that was being attacked by the entire flock. On me and around me came a continual shower of cones until the snow-covered ground

The highly specialized bill of this red crossbill allows it to strip the seeds from a hemlock cone efficiently.

In winters when the crop of northern tree seeds fails, white-winged crossbills irrupt south into the United States in search of food.

was thick with them," he related. "Watching these gorgeous raspberry-colored birds cracking open cones while they hung like little parrots from the terminal branches of snow-laden hemlocks was an experience I shall long remember."

When trees on their northern breeding grounds produce bumper seed crops, grosbeaks and crossbills usually remain there throughout the year. But when the seed crop fails, every two to three years, or when the nesting season has been so productive that competition for food becomes keen, the birds move southward and eastward, well into the United States, in search of food.

Roving for Survival

The erratic migration of the winter finches is their way of coping with a sporadic food supply, according to the Cornell Laboratory of Ornithology (*Newsletter for Members,* Winter, 1978). "It is an adaptation that enables these birds to wander widely until they find their food and, having found it, to stop." During winters when they roam, we have a better chance of seeing these birds, and of hosting those species that will eat sunflower seeds at backyard feeders.

"The extent to which an irruptive finch will wander for food is best shown by the evening grosbeak, which breeds in the coniferous forests to the north and moves south during the winter," the Cornell newsletter explained. "At a site in Pennsylvania, some 17,000 evening grosbeaks were banded over a period of 14 years. Of 499 later recovered, only 48 had returned to the same place in subsequent winters; but 451 others were scattered among 17 states and four Canadian provinces," the authors noted. "These recoveries show both how widely individual grosbeaks range and the weakness of their tendency to return to the same place in later years."

In Rhinelander, Wisconsin, Konnie Hunter has fed evening grosbeaks at her home every winter for the last seventeen years. "They eat five to six pounds of sunflower seeds a day," Konnie told us. "Last winter I fed them twelve hundred pounds during the period they were here, from October to May," she said. At sunrise on a March morning last year, we estimated that there were at least three hundred evening grosbeaks on Konnie's feeders and queuing up on her deck and in the nearby trees waiting for their turn at the banquet.

Feeding Atmosphere Affects Personality

Though they are sociable birds, evening grosbeaks are not necessarily compatible when they are hungry and conditions are crowded at a feeding tray. "There they are often selfish, hostile and belligerent, pushing their way in, sparring with open beaks, and threatening to attack or drive out a new arrival," ornithologist Arthur Cleveland Bent declared. "They are bosses of the tray and are intolerant of other species, driving away even the starlings; only the blue jay seems able to cope with them. Even the females of their own species are not immune

An invasion of evening grosbeaks at a backyard feeder can easily consume five pounds of sunflower seeds in a single day.

to attack by the males," he said. "But so eager are they for their food that the tray remains crowded full of birds as long as there is standing room."

Toward humans, these birds often seem unafraid, perhaps because they are not used to associating with people in their native northern coniferous forests.

The cardinal, which, unlike the grosbeaks and crossbills, breeds in a more southern range and is often in close association with people, is just the opposite. It is rarely tame at feeding stations and seems particularly wary in the northern extensions of its range.

Cardinals may or may not be gregarious, depending on where they live. A single pair of cardinals has established a feeding and breeding territory in our backyard which they protect aggressively against other cardinals throughout the year. Farther south, sixty or more often gather into large flocks. Around Cincinnati, Ohio, cardinals winter in flocks of hundreds, which is why Cincinnati is known as the Cardinal Capital of the World.

Downy Coats and Padded Feet

Like all birds of winter, the large-billed finches are well equipped to withstand the cold, for beneath their contour plumage is a lining of warm down. Their feet, too, can handle wintry conditions. The undersides of the feet, including the toes, are padded in ridges, giving a firm grip on icy branches. "Grosbeaks are outfitted with their own snow tires," quipped one birder.

The northern cardinal prefers sunflower seed feeders that provide substantial footing.

THE BIG FINCHES OF WINTER

Northern Cardinal—An 8-inch bright red finch with a conspicuous crest and black face, the male northern cardinal is the all-time favorite backyard bird. The female is also lovely, light brown to gray with patches of red on her wings, tail, and crest. Cardinals have strong, sharp, cone-shaped red bills. Both sexes whistle a loud, clear and melodious *what cheer! what cheer! purty, purty, purty,* though the female's is somewhat softer. Another call is *cue, cue, cue.* The cardinal is a southern species which has extended its range north into the Great Lakes states, New England, and southern Canada. It lives in dense thickets, parks, and suburban gardens. In winter, its natural food is the seeds and buds of trees and shrubs. At feeding stations, it is especially fond of sunflower seeds and cracked corn. The cardinal is the state bird of Illinois, Indiana, Kentucky, North Carolina, Ohio, Virginia, and West Virginia.

Pine Grosbeak—The largest member of the grosbeak family, the plump pine grosbeak is about 9 inches long. The male has a rose-colored head, back, breast, and rump; tail and wings are black, with two white bars on each wing, and the heavy, conical bill is dark. The female is generally grayish, the rose of the male's head replaced by olive green on hers. The pine grosbeak's call is a sweet, melodious *tee-tee-tew* warble. In winter, the pine grosbeak can be found in open coniferous forests and open juniper and cedar fields where berries can be gleaned, or in fruit-bearing shrubs and trees in backyards and gardens north of the snow line across the United States. It eats the seeds of ash, birches, larch, and various evergreens, plus the fruits of trees, vines and shrubs. It does not normally visit feeding stations.

Red Crossbill—A 6½-inch brick-red bird with a carmine rump and blackish wings, the male red crossbill is a strong contrast to the female, a nondescript bird with an olive wash. Both birds have the characteristic crossed bills, which are indicative of their highly specialized feeding technique for gleaning the seeds of coniferous trees. Red crossbills often feed quietly but may mutter or twitter softly. In flight, they may call a series of *jip* notes. Their winter ranges are erratic. As authority Robert Lemmon noted, they may be in the coniferous forests of the Georgia mountains in summer and Quebec in winter, or vice versa. Their natural winter diet is almost entirely tree seeds, particularly those of evergreens. They do not normally patronize feeding stations.

White-winged Crossbill—A pinkish red bird with a black tail and two white wing bars across each black wing, the 6½-inch male is similar to, but smaller than, a male pine grosbeak. The females of the two species are also similar in their olive-gray plumage with washes of yellow on the rump, breast, and sides. The distinctive crossed bill is the infallible field mark. The call of the white-winged crossbill is a *chif-chif,* or a sweet *peet.* Its winter range is erratic, from the boreal forests of the far north southward to the snow line across the United States. Like the red crossbill's, its winter food is chiefly coniferous tree seeds. The white-winged does not normally use feeding stations.

Evening Grosbeak—Few winter birds are as exciting to watch as the male evening grosbeak, a plump 8-inch yellow, brown, and white bird with black wings. The female is similar but duller, feathered in gray tinged with yellow. Both have heavy whitish green bills. Prominent white patches on the wings effect a showy flight. Misnamed because of the old belief that they feed only at sundown, evening grosbeaks are noisy birds that call a ringing *clee-ip.* In winter they are erratic and may travel south into the United States, sometimes south of the snow line; they may be found in coniferous forests, where they eat the seeds of spruce, fir, maple, ash, and box elder. They have a liking for salt and are often seen along roadsides where salt has been used during winter. They are well known for their assaults on backyard sunflower seed feeders.

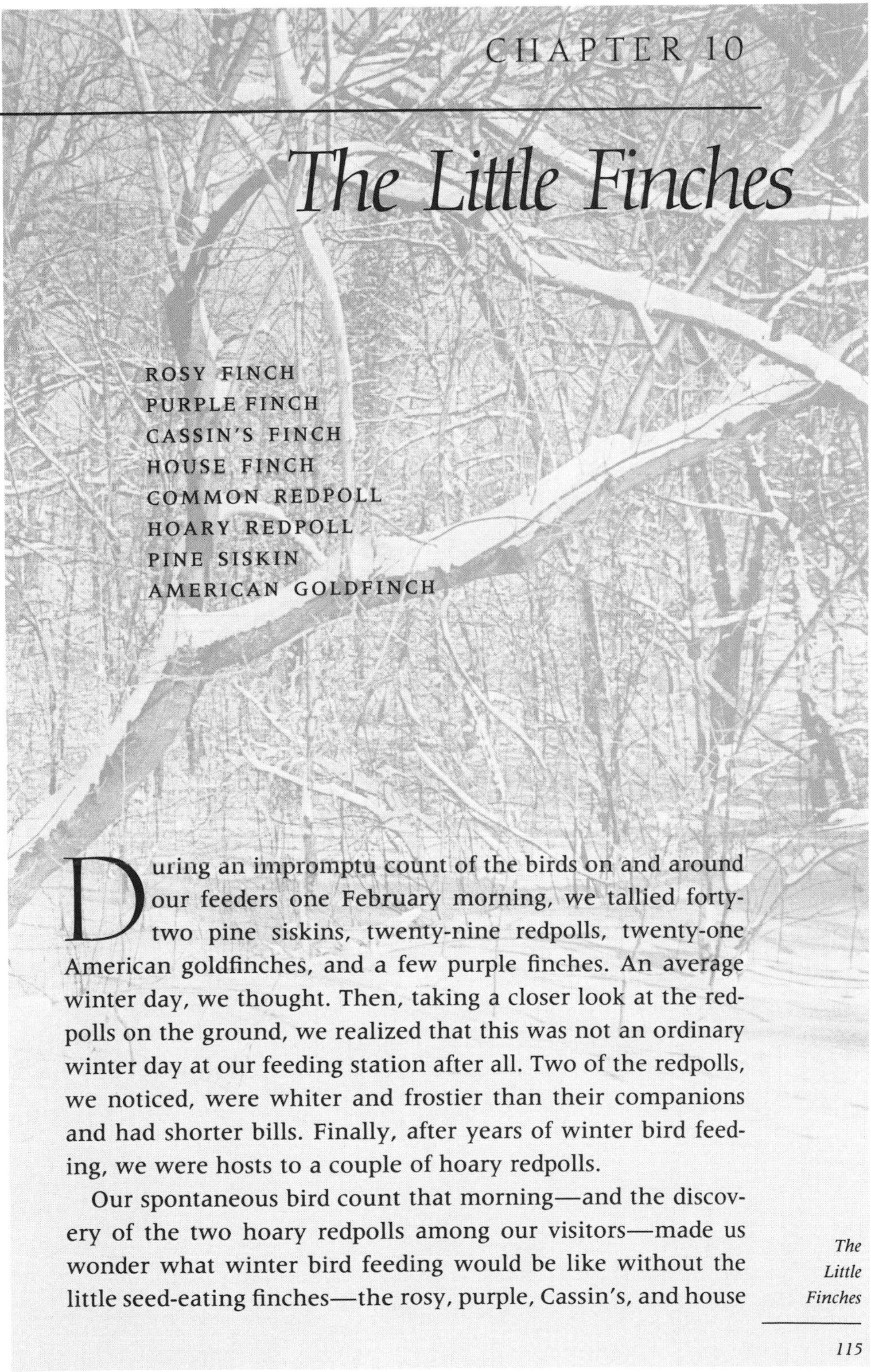

CHAPTER 10

The Little Finches

ROSY FINCH
PURPLE FINCH
CASSIN'S FINCH
HOUSE FINCH
COMMON REDPOLL
HOARY REDPOLL
PINE SISKIN
AMERICAN GOLDFINCH

During an impromptu count of the birds on and around our feeders one February morning, we tallied forty-two pine siskins, twenty-nine redpolls, twenty-one American goldfinches, and a few purple finches. An average winter day, we thought. Then, taking a closer look at the red-polls on the ground, we realized that this was not an ordinary winter day at our feeding station after all. Two of the redpolls, we noticed, were whiter and frostier than their companions and had shorter bills. Finally, after years of winter bird feeding, we were hosts to a couple of hoary redpolls.

Our spontaneous bird count that morning—and the discovery of the two hoary redpolls among our visitors—made us wonder what winter bird feeding would be like without the little seed-eating finches—the rosy, purple, Cassin's, and house

Because their bills are much smaller than those of cardinals and grosbeaks, common redpolls prefer hulled sunflower seeds or smaller seeds.

finches, redpolls, pine siskins, and American goldfinches. It would be much less exciting, certainly, because these tiny birds usually provide the great numbers—and often the color—that make feeding birds in winter such a joy.

Though each is a separate species among the world's twelve hundred finches, these very hardy birds of winter have a great deal in common. The most obvious link is their diet. In winter, they subsist on the small seeds of trees, shrubs, and weeds.

Each is a common visitor at feeding stations in some region of the continent. In fact, house finches in the Southwest and common redpolls in Alaska are at the top of the list of birds that visit feeders in those regions, according to data gathered by the Cornell Laboratory of Ornithology's Project Feeder-Watch. House finches, pine siskins, and American goldfinches are among the top five in other regions of the continent.

If You See One, You'll See a Dozen

These diminutive seed-eating finches are quite gregarious in winter, probably for reasons of survival. Rarely will you see just one house finch, or a lone goldfinch, or a solitary pine sis-

American goldfinches in their drab winter plumage enjoy a meal of hulled sunflower seeds.

kin. Typically there will be a dozen or more feeding in coniferous woodlands, open fields, or alpine terraces, depending on the species.

Where there is sufficient food and feeding space, their gregariousness motivates them to assemble in immense flocks. During 1988–89, one respondent in Project FeederWatch reported that there were 234 goldfinches at his feeders at one time.

This flocking habit means there is likely to be squabbling and fighting over feeding space—customary behavior among all the finches when they are concentrated at feeders. Aggressive behavior is most often the trademark of pine siskins and house finches as each bird claims a couple of square inches of feeding tray for its own . . . and woe betide the bird that tries to encroach.

Even at night finches are gregarious. Flocks of rosy finches use the same roosting site throughout the winter, arriving in midafternoon as daylight begins to wane. Their roost is usually a great outcropping of rock with many cracks and indentations into which they can tuck themselves to get out of the wind,

Flocks of rosy finches usually roost in an outcropping of rock where they can get out of the cold wind.

but they have also been known to roost in the abandoned mud nests of cliff-swallow colonies.

House finches seek the overhanging eaves of buildings, vines growing on walls, and nooks in buildings for roosts. Although purple finches may use buidlings, too, more often they roost in dense evergreen thickets, as do goldfinches.

But occasionally a bird must settle for whatever it can find for shelter when darkness approaches. At sunset on a late January day, Dr. Charles Townsend found a goldfinch anxiously flitting about a small pine grove in Massachusetts, alighting at the bases of trees and eventually popping into a hole about a foot deep in the snow under a stump. "Frightened from there, it flew about nervously for a few minutes," Dr. Townsend related. "It finally cuddled into the protected side of a footprint in the snow." It was evident that the goldfinch had been searching for a protected hole in which to pass the night, and Townsend speculated that the bird considered the footprint a safe place because the snow in that region showed no sign of prowling animals.

A Bonanza of Bold Birds

At sunrise, the birds are roving the countryside again in search of food, some heading straight for backyard feeding stations. Many of the species that normally have no contact with humans on their remote breeding grounds in the far north are

Birds of the boreal forests, common redpolls irregularly irrupt south into the United States to find their winter food of seeds and cones.

often quite bold at feeders. Artist Tom Rost of Cedarburg, Wisconsin, found this to be true of pine siskins. One winter when there was a major invasion of the little striped finches, he had to fill the feeders outside his studio window several times a day. By the end of January, the siskins had become so tame that they came when he called to them, took niger seed from his hand, and swarmed over him when he poured seed into the feeders.

The favorite feeding-station food, not only for siskins, but among all of these smaller finches, is niger seed, erroneously called thistle seed by many people. Niger is best presented in special tube feeders with tiny ports just large enough to allow a bird to extract one seed at a time.

Aside from the popularity of niger among the finches, another plus is that many of the "less desirable" bird species do not fancy niger and leave it alone. In addition, the minute holes in niger seed feeders limit use by birds with larger, less pointed bills.

The little finches also relish sunflower seeds. Given a choice, they prefer it hulled (out of the shells and broken into bits) because the large, hard shells of the striped sunflower seeds are more difficult for the small-billed finches to crack. Martha and D. F. Balph of the University of Utah, who studied pine siskin behavior at feeders, reported, "When evening grosbeaks ate gray-striped sunflower seeds, siskins—which have difficulty opening these thick-hulled seeds—often tried to defend the area under a grosbeak's bill where bits of seed dropped to the ground." The smaller and more nutritious black oil sunflower seed, on the other hand, is easier than the striped sunflower seed for the siskins to open, so it is the better choice for attracting these birds.

Other seeds that the finches eat at feeding stations include red and white proso millet and hemp.

When not gorging themselves at feeding stations, these little finches are foraging in the countryside for the natural foods that have sustained them for eons. Because their bills are much smaller than those of cardinals and grosbeaks, their natural foods are the smaller tree seeds such as those from elm, white ash, red maple, and alder, plus the so-called weed seeds from a host of perennial grasses and native plants.

The purple finch moves south from its northern coniferous habitat in winter, frequenting backyards that offer sunflower and niger seeds.

Many of these finches are also attracted to salt. They are occasionally seen congregating on the shoulders of roads where salt has been applied during winter, at salt licks, and on bare ground where salt has been poured.

Food Supply Governs Migration

Food, in fact, is an overriding influence in the lives of these stalwart small fry. If provisions are not abundant in the coniferous forests, open fields, or alpine slopes where they nest, they must move to other regions of the continent, usually south, but sometimes east or west, where food is plentiful. These erratic migrations, or irruptions, among wandering finches are unpredictable.

For example, "The pine siskin, normally a northern species, launched a massive invasion to all corners of North America during the winter of 1987–88," Erica H. Dunn, coordinator of the Cornell Laboratory of Ornithology's Project FeederWatch, reported. It was estimated that there were, at the very least, ninety-five million pine siskins at feeders throughout North America that February. "The winter of 1988–89 brought a radically different picture, however, as siskins seemed to disappear from many regions," Dunn added.

At least ninety-five million pine siskins visited North American backyard feeders during February a few years ago.

Why the difference? There is no absolute answer, but studies of the feeding habits of pine siskins indicate that during the winter of 1987–88, a food scarcity on their home range must have forced them to irrupt into most of the United States, as far south as the Gulf Coast. In 1988–89, food conditions on their home range apparently improved significantly and the birds were not required to wander widely. They did not show up at bird-feeding stations in nearly the numbers of a year earlier (they were down 99 percent in the Southeast).

Dunn points out that irruption is a risky business for the finches because the chances of mortality increase with any kind of long-distance movement. "Still, if there is no food at home, birds that leave in search of other food may have a better chance of survival," says Dunn. "It's possible that bird feeders, by providing irruptive species with a stable food supply, may be improving the odds of survival for these species."

LITTLE FINCHES OF WINTER

Rosy Finch—A chunky, 6-inch sparrowlike bird, the pinkish brown male has a gray or brown cap and a black forehead. Females are duller and grayer. Their call is a series of high-pitched *cheews*. In flight, flocks utter a *pert-pert-chew*. There are eight subspecies of rosy finches, and until recently, four were recognized as separate species: the gray-cheeked, or Hepburn's, rosy finch, the gray-crowned rosy finch, the black rosy finch, and the brown-capped rosy finch. These birds live in the rocky

A bird of the Rocky Mountain alpine tundra, the rosy finch is usually forced to lower altitudes in winter, when it regularly shows up in backyards looking for seeds.

outcrops of alpine tundra in the Rocky Mountains, where they eat seeds of weeds found on the steep slopes of canyon walls. Extreme winter weather will eventually drive them to lower altitudes and often to feeding stations, where they eat niger and hulled sunflower seeds. They can also be attracted to salt.

Purple Finch—The color of the 6-inch male purple finch is closer to raspberry or old rose than to purple. Its coloring is brightest on the head and rump, with a conspicuous splash on the breast. The female looks like a brown-striped sparrow with a white eye line. The flight call is a sharp *pit* or *tick.* In winter, purple finches move from their northern coniferous-forest habitat south into the United States. In some years, they wander well below the snow line to Baja and the mountains of southern Arizona in the West and to the Gulf Coast and Florida in the East. They feed on tree, weed, and grass seeds, as well as tree buds, and visit feeding stations for sunflower and niger seeds. The purple finch is New Hampshire's state bird.

Cassin's Finch—This 6-inch purple finch look-alike has a paler throat and breast, and a red cap that ends sharply at its brown-streaked nape and back. Females and immature birds mirror their purple finch counterparts. The Cassin's call is a clear three-note *cheep;* in flight, it is *dee-up.* This bird of the high, semiarid, coniferous forests of the West may remain in the higher mountains throughout the year but is frequently encountered at feeding stations at lower elevations in the foothills and valleys in winter. Its natural winter food is buds, berries, and seeds, particularly those of conifers.

House Finch—At first glance, the 5½-inch male house finch, with its striped flanks and bright red forehead, bib, and rump, looks very much like a purple or Cassin's finch, but it is smaller and more streamlined and lacks the distinct ear patch and eyebrow. Females are gray-brown above and striped below. The call is a hoarse *wheer* or *che-urr,* and sometimes a musical chirping. The house finch's historical range was the western third of the United States, but in 1940, cage-bird dealers on Long Island, having received the birds illegally from California suppliers, released their house finches to avoid prosecution for having the wild birds in captivity. The species has now extended its range throughout the East and is soon expected to meet its western brethren somewhere east of the Rockies. This very aggressive and gregarious bird eats almost any vegetable matter, though it prefers seeds, particularly hemp seeds. It commonly raids feeding stations in large flocks.

The very aggressive and gregarious house finch has become a pest at many eastern feeding stations.

Common Redpoll—A bright red cap, black chin patch, and streaked grayish brown underparts distinguish this 5-inch finch. The male typically has a rosy red breast and sides. The call is a trilling *chet-chet-chet-chet* or a twittering. This bird of the boreal forest irregularly irrupts into the United States in search of its winter diet of seeds and cones of birch, alder, willow, pine, elm, and basswood.

Hoary Redpoll—The hoary is almost identical with the common redpoll in appearance, call, and diet, but it has a lighter, frosty appearance and smaller bill. It is sometimes identified among common redpolls at feeding stations.

Pine Siskin—These heavily streaked 4½-inch brown finches with yellow wing and tail patches are irregular visitors to the

United States in winter. A wheezing *tee-ee* or a rising *shreeeh* is heard while the birds are feeding, often in the company of American goldfinches and common redpolls. Their natural winter foods are the seeds of coniferous trees, alder, birch, and ragweed. They are also attracted to salt. Large flocks of pine siskins may invade backyard feeding stations across the northern United States, south to the Gulf Coast and into Mexico.

American Goldfinch—In winter this 5-inch "wild canary" is olive gray, a drastic change from the male's bright yellow and jet-black summer plumage. The sexes look alike in winter, with darker wings and white wing bars. A canarylike twittering and a plaintive *se-weee*, slurring upward at the end, are heard from the goldfinch throughout the winter, as is the familiar *per-chik-o-ree* flight call. The goldfinch's winter range extends from the farmlands, parks, and suburbs of southern Canada and the northern United States to the Gulf Coast and Mexico. Its natural winter diet is seeds of sunflower, thistle, ragweed, gray birch, and alder. At feeding stations, it enjoys niger and sunflower seeds. It is the state bird of Iowa, New Jersey, and Washington.

CHAPTER 11

Larks, Juncos, Sparrows, and Buntings

HORNED LARK
SONG SPARROW
AMERICAN TREE SPARROW
WHITE-THROATED SPARROW
WHITE-CROWNED SPARROW
DARK-EYED JUNCO
LAPLAND LONGSPUR
SNOW BUNTING

In the depths of a northern winter, when the temperatures are well below zero and the wind is howling at 35 mph, the windchill factor may be −50°F.

It was just such a day that we chose for a February drive along a rural road in east-central Wisconsin near Horicon National Wildlife Refuge. With a foot of snow on the ground, and more of it streaming across the road in front of us like strands of white hair blowing in the west wind, it was a day that most would agree wasn't "fit for man nor beast."

We forged on in the hope of seeing some sign of life in the white wasteland of flat farm fields, broken only by the occasional house and barn. There was no apparent life out there, in this season, in this desolate landscape of ice and snow. Yet there was life out there for those who knew where to look, for

Larks, Juncos, Sparrows, and Buntings

The arrival of snow buntings early in the winter is believed to be a precursor of bad weather.

American tree sparrows consumed an estimated 875 tons of weed seeds each winter in Iowa, a nineteenth-century authority claimed.

this was the time of the "snowbirds," the most stout-hearted birds of winter.

Suddenly we spotted what we had been seeking—a flock of snow buntings, Lapland longspurs, and a few horned larks, all foraging along the roadside for waste grain from farm trucks, or possibly for road salt.

Life on the Snow

Thriving in a winter environment unsuitable for many other birds, these snowbirds—along with the American tree sparrow, white-throated sparrow, white-crowned sparrow, and dark-eyed junco—have a great deal in common. The most prominent trait is that they are mostly ground-feeding birds—even the American tree sparrow, which was misnamed by the early settlers, who saw a resemblance to the tree sparrow of Europe, a chestnut-capped species that does live in trees.

Each species in this group spends most of the winter on the ground in a habitat of open farm fields, barren plains, meadows, deserts, beaches, golf courses, and sand dunes. They sur-

The dark-eyed junco is the most widespread feeding-station species in North America.

vive winter with little or no cover, using depressions in the exposed landscape to shield them from the wind.

The snow bunting, for example, the epitome of the winter snowbird, is seen only in the most open country. "The ground is their accustomed haunt for both feeding and sleeping, for back home they never saw a real tree and never think of alighting in one when they go traveling," bird authority Robert Lemmon points out.

Food = Fat = Heat

Perhaps the most amazing thing about this robust group of little birds is their ability to stay warm in horrendous cold. "Juncos lay down a layer of fat for the winter," says naturalist Jean George of the dark-eyed junco. "The fat usually serves a dual function. It insulates, and is burned to provide heat." During a cold night, the birds will burn off 12 to 15 percent of their body weight just to keep warm. Without abundant food to promptly regain weight, the birds would die of starvation. That

Sometimes in winter the familiar Old Sam Peabody, Peabody *song of the white-throated sparrow may be heard.*

Unlike other sparrows, which enjoy the company of mixed flocks, the white-crowned sparrow remains aloof.

is why they feed most actively at sunrise and again just before dark.

At night, they use the most basic shelters for roosts. Snow buntings, which can stand temperatures below −40°F, crouch close together beside clods of dirt or in crevices in rocks, or sometimes burrow into snow. Tree sparrows seek weedy fields or cattail marshes, where each bird tucks itself into a little crevice on or near the ground for protection against the elements.

All of these snowbirds are gregarious, both among their own kind and with the others in this group. Apparently they find safety and improved foraging when they gather in large groups.

In general, they also communicate continually. "One of the most pleasant events in the white-throats' winter days is the sociable way a group of them will gather for the night in an accustomed sleeping retreat," Lemmon remarked. "Evergreen

Larks,
Juncos,
Sparrows,
and
Buntings

hedges are favorite spots, and here you will hear their distinctive chinking chorus as dusk begins. Sometimes, too, there will be a snatch of song," he pointed out. "And finally, with the coming of darkness, a keen ear may catch the low, companionable murmurings with which they settle down for the night."

Weed Seeds Top the List

These birds are ardent seed eaters, but as ground feeders, they are not as interested in tree seeds as are finches, grosbeaks, and crossbills. They generally seek seeds that grow in farm fields, grasslands, and open parklands. In fact, the tree sparrow's diet is 98 percent weed seeds. F.E.L. Beal, a nineteenth-century authority on the diets of birds, declared that in the state of Iowa alone, tree sparrows consumed 875 tons of weed seeds each winter.

A dark-eyed junco forages on the ground in winter by giving a double shuffle with spread feet and a quick jump backward to throw the snow behind it and uncover seeds beneath.

Nearly all of the members of this group forage on the ground in winter in the same manner—by scratching the snow with their feet to uncover the seeds hidden beneath. When white-throated sparrows are searching for food, they give a triple shuffle with spread feet, and a quick jump backward to throw out the dirt or snow behind them. They will continue scratching for up to an hour, pausing only to pick up the food they uncover.

Reliable Migrants

As a group, these birds are also predictable migrators, both to their breeding grounds in the far north and to their wintering grounds in southern Canada and the northern United States.

Snow buntings travel the farthest. Birds of land's last outpost on the arctic tundra, they journey southward in large flocks, resembling the large flakes of snow they seem to bring with them. They seldom drift south of the northern tiers of the United States, content to stoically glean seeds from weeds that are exposed above the snow. Then, with the first warmth of

With white tail feathers flashing, the dark-eyed junco flies north to breed when the last threat of snow has passed.

early spring, the wayfarers vanish as abruptly as they came, heading north.

In some regions of the country, the arrival of snow buntings early in the season suggests there has been an early and intense winter to the north, and that is a precursor of bad weather locally. The same is true of the dark-eyed junco, the species most commonly nicknamed the "snowbird." As surely as the sun rises, we will see the first dark-eyed junco in Wisconsin during the first week of October, reminding us that the first snow of the season is not far off. And when the last threat of snow passes in the spring, the last little snowbird disappears with it.

In snow-covered farm fields, the horned lark feeds on waste grain and weed seeds.

THE SNOWBIRDS OF WINTER

Horned Lark—A generally brownish, streaked and spotted 7¼-inch bird that blends with its surroundings, the horned lark is well named. Both sexes sport black feathered adornments on the sides of their heads that may be raised to look like horns. The male's markings are more vivid than the female's, and his horns are more conspicuous. Their call is a squeaking *tsee-teetee,* or a *ti-sick*. In its winter habitat of farm fields, beaches, and sand dunes throughout the United States, it feeds on waste grain and weed seeds. It often nests in February, even in the North, when snow is still present.

Song Sparrow—A heavily streaked breast with a large central breast spot are the key markings of the 6-inch song sparrow. Sexes look alike. The song sparrow's call or alarm note is a loud *chimp*, but its song on the first warm day of spring is a most welcome *sweet, sweet,* followed by a jumble of notes of various tones. Song sparrows are found on farms and in cities and suburbs, usually on the ground, where they can forage for

Song sparrows spend the winter quietly scratching for a living of seeds beneath backyard feeders, but come spring, they fill the air with their sweet songs.

weed seeds, fruits, and berries. Bird seeds at ground feeders and water in ponds will attract song sparrows to backyards in winter.

American Tree Sparrow—A central black breast spot stands out like a badge on the plain grayish breast of this 6-inch bird. It has a bright and clean chestnut cap, and two white bars decorate each dusky brown wing. The sexes are similar in appearance. Their call note is a soft *tsip*, but by February they are tuning up with their sping trill. In their winter habitat of weedy fields, marshes, and suburban gardens across the northern tiers of the United States, they eat small seeds and are steady customers at backyard feeders.

White-throated Sparrow—The distinct white throat patch, the yellow mark between the bill and eye, and the flatter head of the white-throated sparrow distinguish this 6½-inch bird from the similar white-crowned sparrow. Adults of both species have black-and-white head stripes. The whitethroat's call note is a *tseet*. Its song, which is sometimes heard in winter, is the pleasing *Old Sam Peabody, Peabody, Peabody*. On its brushland winter habitat, from New England west to the Great Lakes and south to Florida and Texas, the bird searches mainly for weed seeds and is a regular visitor at feeding stations.

White-crowned Sparrow—The fluffy, dome-shaped head and white crown of this 7-inch bird differ from the flatter head of the white-throated sparrow. Its call note is *tsit,* but in late winter it may sing a few sharp whistles followed by a trill. In its Northeast and Northwest winter habitat of brushy fencerows and suburban shrubbery, it eats seeds of weeds and grasses, as well as feeding-station offerings.

Dark-eyed Junco—In the East, this 6-inch bird is slate-colored with a gray vest, sharply defined by an abrupt line where the white underparts begin. In the West, it has a black head and brown body. The females are brownish and their vests are less sharply marked. White outer tail feathers flash as the bird fans its tail in flight. Its call note is *tchet, tchet,* or *tack, tack,* or *clink.* Its winter habitat of brushy woods, weedy fields, and gardens across all of the United States and southern Canada provides a diet of seeds from small trees and weeds. This species is the most widespread feeding-station species in North America.

Lapland Longspur—In winter, the 6½-inch Lapland longspur has a brown back streaked with black. Its underparts are light, the abdomen is streaked with brown, there are two white wing bars, and the nape is faintly chestnut. The black throat and breast and the bright chestnut nape are acquired in the spring.

The Lapland longspur typically feeds quietly on the ground and may go unnoticed unless it is flushed.

The female is less distinctly marked. Its call is a plaintive *teew,* or a dry rattle followed by a whistle. In its winter habitat in fields, plains, and prairies across southern Canada and the northern tiers of the United States, the bird feeds on seeds and waste grain. It is not likely to visit backyard feeding stations.

Snow Bunting—No other songbird is as white as this one. In overhead flight, the 6½-inch snow bunting shows none of the brown that streaks the white upperparts, and it appears to be pure white. Females are duller than the males. Their call note is a twittering, or a sweet *chirrup.* In a winter habitat of snow-covered, usually treeless, open country, the snow bunting forages for seeds of weeds poking through the snow, and occasionally patronizes bird feeders. It winters across southern Canada and in the northern tier of the United States.

CHAPTER 12

The Immigrants

EUROPEAN STARLING
HOUSE SPARROW

W hile a downy woodpecker quietly fed at the suet feeder on the trunk of the basswood tree, three European starlings crashed the serenity, attacked the downy at the suet, and drove the panicked woodpecker into flight.

At about the same time, a swarm of fifteen house sparrows descended on the feeding tray, causing chaos among the foragers and flushing away the small flock of dark-eyed juncos and tree sparrows.

Like them or not, these two foreigners—the European starling and the house sparrow—are aggressive survivors of the first order and are certainly among the most indomitable birds of winter. Labeled pests by nearly everyone who feeds birds, these outsiders have carved a niche for themselves in "the land of the free and the home of the brave."

Though they are unrelated and very different in appearance, they have plenty in common, particularly in winter. Both are gregarious, forming large winter flocks for feeding and roosting. In winter, both may seek warmth from chimneys of houses or office buidlings. Both are aggressive toward native species, both are frequent visitors to bird-feeding stations, both eat grain and beef suet, and both are more common in urban areas than in suburban backyards.

In its speckled winter garb, the aggressive European starling is an unwelcome intruder at many feeding stations.

The European starling, an immigrant during the late nineteenth century, is among the least popular birds in North America, aggressively displacing many native birds from feeding and breeding sites. Common flickers have tried to nest in a flicker house on our terrace at least a dozen times, only to be driven away by pairs of starlings which, having successfully fended off the flickers, eventually abandoned the house.

In late fall, the starling's iridescent black and dark green

The Immigrants

breeding plumage is replaced by speckled garb, giving the bird a completely different appearance.

At about the same time, starlings congregate in huge flocks. As the autumn leaves fall, the birds abandon their tree roosts for the warmer cover provided by city buidlings, church steeples, and the eaves of houses. Starling flocks are noisy and dirty and present a formidable problem for the owners of those buildings. Many schemes—incorporating baffles, electrified wires, and chemicals—have been instituted to discourage the birds from roosting in man-made structures, but without much success.

The house sparrow has a similar history in North America. In the mid-1800s, house sparrows trapped in Europe were released in the United States, most notably in the Brooklyn, New York, area, to establish a population of house sparrows in America. A few homesick Europeans simply missed their *sputzies;* others wanted to introduce to America every bird that Shakespeare mentioned. Still others believed that house sparrows, by feasting on cankerworms, elm spanworms, Japanese beetles, and other harmful insects and their larvae, would be a

Not a true sparrow, the gregarious house sparrow forages in winter flocks on farmlands and in urban backyards throughout North America.

boon to agriculture. It is true that they eat many of these insect pests, but the trade-off was not worth it. Like starlings, house sparrows forced out some of our native species, including bluebirds, chickadees, titmice, and woodpeckers, from feeding, roosting, and nesting sites.

The house sparrow, or English sparrow, is not a sparrow at all but a member of the Old World family of weaverbirds, or weaver finches, most of which are much more colorful and attractive than the house sparrow.

Strangely, the house sparrow's greatest threat is from the European starling, with which it vies somewhat unsuccessfully for nesting cavities in spring and for space on bird feeders in winter.

The other house sparrow equalizer is the automobile. From the bird's introduction into North America until the early part of the twentieth century, the house sparrow thrived on the waste grain and straw seeds found in the horse barns of every community. But with the change of private transportation from horses to cars, house sparrow numbers declined dramatically. Today, house sparrows are still numerous in the centers of cities, where they compete with rock doves (pigeons) for food, and around farm operations, where they still find waste grain.

If the starling and house sparrow are problems at backyard feeding stations, a "nuisance" feeder might be tried, suggests Richard M. DeGraaf, a U.S. Forest Service researcher at the University of Massachusetts. Set a feeding tray on a five-foot-high post and locate it about thirty feet out on the lawn, away from window feeders. This setup is supposed to be particularly attractive to these two species of birds.

THE STARLING AND HOUSE SPARROW OF WINTER

European Starling—In winter, the short-tailed, long-billed, 8-inch European starling has a speckled plumage and brownish bill, very different from its summer outfit of glossy black and a distinct yellow bill. Introduced into North America in New York City in 1890, it quickly spread and is now a pest throughout the continent. Its winter calls vary from squeaks and chirps to sharp whistles and twittering. Starlings winter in large flocks in cities, farmlands, and open woodlands, often with grackles and blackbirds, searching for fruits, grains, and, at feeding stations, beef suet and seed.

House Sparrow—The winter plumage of the 6-inch male house sparrow is brown-gray with a chestnut-streaked back and faint black bib, which becomes more vivid in spring. The female is a plain little brown bird with a streaked back. Their call is a monotonous *chit-chup*. In winter, house sparrows are common near farmlands, where flocks feed on grain. They are pests at feeding stations.

CHAPTER 13

Attracting the Birds of Winter

P eering through the picture windows of our home in mid-winter is like looking upon a Christmas card landscape come to life. Next to the pond, heavy snow burdens the white pine and Norway spruce, their dense boughs drooping toward the ground. The yews and creeping juniper on the other side are buried, except for several tunnellike entrances leading to dark retreats under the sparkling white blanket.

The snowy setting is serene, yet very much alive with the color and movement of the birds of winter. On a typical day, a flock of two dozen evening grosbeaks will gorge themselves on sunflower seeds from a variety of feeders. Chickadees and nut-hatches flit to and from a sunflower seed feeder hanging from a tree limb. Meanwhile, nearly thirty goldfinches, dressed in

From our sunroom, we enjoy watching the winter birds that frequent our feeders and find cover in our recycled Christmas tree.

their drab olive winter plumage, remove niger seeds from other hanging tube feeders.

On the feeding tray in the center of the scene, a pair of cardinals, three blue jays, and several more evening grosbeaks provide colorful accents. Juncos, sparrows, and mourning doves feed contentedly on the wild bird seed mix scattered on top of the snow.

A male downy woodpecker and a female hairy woodpecker complete the picture as they work both sides of the beef suet feeder on the trunk of the ash tree.

Establishing the Essential Elements

What we see is tremendously rewarding—a classic backyard sanctuary for the birds of winter.

How did we achieve it? It really wasn't difficult or expensive; we simply provided the elements that wild birds require of their winter habitat.

American goldfinches are among the dozen or so species that commonly visit feeders in a successful backyard wildlife habitat.

Many books have been written about how to attract birds to backyards, including our own *The Backyard Bird Watcher.* The information contained in all those books can be summed up in three little words: *cover, food,* and *water.*

Any backyard that provides an adequate amount of these three essential wildlife requirements will have birds in winter as well as the other seasons. It is also likely to support an interesting variety of other forms of wildlife—squirrels, chipmunks, raccoons, opossums, skunks, and rabbits, for example, and, in summer, snakes, toads, butterflies, and moths, too.

Cover:

Of the three habitat elements essential for survival, cover—trees, shrubs, and low-growing plants—is the most important.

Dense cover, like that furnished by evergreens, is more crucial to many birds in winter than during other seasons because it will shield them from harsh winter winds, subzero temperatures, falling snow, and freezing rain.

In winter, deciduous trees, such as maples, oaks, birches, and beeches, are naked skeletons at a time when the need for suitable cover is critical. But evergreens, such as pines, spruces, cedars, and yews, retain their needles throughout the year, giving the birds of winter superb cover against severe weather, as well as hiding places and escape routes from both winged and four-footed predators.

Instant cover. Not every backyard has an abundance of evergreens, and it may be costly to plant them and it could take

These woodpeckers, downy and pileated, would not feed in this backyard if they did not have adequate natural cover, including mature trees.

years for them to attain a size that would be useful to birds. There is a way, however, to have instant evergreens. By collecting discarded Christmas trees and placing them where cover is needed, a landowner can transform a backyard into a winter bird paradise in a few minutes. The Christmas trees can be tied to posts or deciduous trees with twine or wire. Or set the tree in a traditional Christmas tree stand, or build a special new stand for it, or wedge it into a concrete block for support.

Christmas trees will be most effective as cover if they are placed near or right against feeding stations, giving the birds easy access to the cover should a predator appear. The trees will also serve as a windbreak for the birds using the feeders.

The Christmas trees should remain fairly green and fresh-looking throughout the remainder of the winter. By the time

Homeowners with backyards that lack adequate plantings can create instant cover by placing discarded Christmas trees near bird feeders.

they turn brown, spring has arrived, and they can be removed and possibly replaced by living trees planted in the same spots.

Big cover. Mature trees are also important if maximum cover is to be offered to winter birds. Large oaks, maples, and hickory trees, for example, will boost the number of species of winter birds that are likely to frequent the property. The tree trunks and heavy branches attract larger winter birds such as pileated, black-backed, and three-toed woodpeckers, and crows, ravens, and jays. Brown creepers and nuthatches will find those same trees perfect for their tree-trunk foraging in search of insect eggs and dormant insect larvae. Cavities in these large trees may serve as roosts for woodpeckers, nuthatches, chickadees, titmice, creepers, and owls. Hawks and owls might be enticed to roost in and to hunt from mature trees. Gallinaceous birds will forage underneath them for seeds and nuts.

Food:

Landowners who plant cover should consider using plant types that also provide natural food for birds. Examples of trees that afford excellent cover as well as natural food include seed- and nut-producing species such as pines, spruces, oaks, beeches, maples, basswoods, hickories, and walnuts. Small trees and shrubs that meet this goal are dogwoods, highbush cranberry, hawthorn, crab apple, and autumn olive. Perennials from which the birds may glean food throughout the winter months include sunflowers, asters, and daisies.

Feeding stations. To satisfy the greatest number and variety of bird species, all of these natural foods can be—and should be—supplemented with an assortment of bird foods presented in various styles of bird feeders at different levels.

Sunflower. If we could offer only one type of food at our own feeding station, it would be sunflower seed. Not only does sunflower seed appeal to such "glamor" species as cardinals, grosbeaks, finches, chickadees, titmice, and nuthatches, but it is very high in protein, giving the birds the highest food value for the money spent.

In the shell, sunflower seeds are available in both the large white-striped and the smaller black oil seed. The smaller oil

Backyard plants that provide birds with both cover and natural food, such as wild grape and crab apple, give the birds two of the three essential elements of a backyard sanctuary.

seed is richer in protein, according to seed authorities, though both kinds are first-class bird food.

Out of the shell, the so-called hulled sunflower, or sunflower meats, are just as popular, particuarly among finches.

Cracked corn. To find out what species eat which bird seeds in the upper Midwest, we conducted a study of the preferences of winter birds in Wisconsin over two winters. The food that attracted the greatest number of species and the greatest number of individuals of those species was cracked corn. This suprises many people who consider cracked corn to be the food only of the less desirable bird species, such as house sparrows, starlings, and pigeons. Those birds do eat cracked corn, but so do chickadees, cardinals, blue jays, and juncos. Next in order of preference to the greatest number of species was sunflower seed, followed by white and red millet.

Interestingly, a friend tried the same experiment in Louisiana and reported that the birds' preferences there were the same as those in the Wisconsin study.

Roosting areas can be provided in backyards by leaving birdhouses out all winter.

Wild bird seed mixes. The results of these studies led to a wild bird seed mixture that is endorsed by and sold at the Schlitz Audubon Center in Milwaukee. The so-called SAC Mix contains only cracked corn, sunflower seeds, and both white and red millet. It contains no filler seeds, such as wheat, buckwheat, and milo, which are found in some wild bird seed mixtures, but which are usually eaten mostly by mice and other rodents at night.

Niger. There is another seed that is very popular with many of the birds of winter, particuarly the finches. It is often called thistle seed, but its real name is niger. This tiny, shiny black seed grows in Ethiopia and India, and is sold in lawn and garden shops, nature centers, and at some feed mills. Niger is expensive, usually costing around one dollar a pound, and for that reason it is also called black gold. But it is very, very popular among the finches—goldfinches, house finches, pine siskins, redpolls—and even chickadees and mourning doves relish a meal of niger seed.

There have been some problems involving the importation of niger. Fearful of inadvertently importing exotic noxious weeds along with the niger, the U.S. Department of Agriculture has required that the seed be sterilized before it is sold in the United States. A few years ago, the sterilization process that was employed destroyed the niger's appeal to birds. People who purchased the seed during that period could not understand why the birds ignored it. For about two years, niger seemed useless.

The current sterilizing method does not affect the seed's ability to attract birds. Once again, niger is tops with the finches.

Beef suet. Another highly effective food for attracting the birds of winter is beef suet, the white fat that surrounds beef kidneys, which is often available free or for a nominal charge at supermarkets and butcher shops, in addition to being sold in cake form at garden and wildlife centers. All woodpeckers, and an assortment of other birds, are potential customers for beef suet at backyard feeding stations. It provides the fat needed to produce body heat, and is an acceptable substitute for the grubs and larvae on which woodpeckers normally dine.

Peanut butter spread on tree bark may attract brown creepers, nuthatches, and woodpeckers in winter.

Feeders for all foods. For each type of bird food there is an appropriate style of feeder. Suet, for example, is best offered in a cagelike feeder, which allows the birds to remove the suet through the wire openings but restricts its wholesale removal by raccoons and other four-legged bird-food robbers.

Niger, a tiny seed, is served to birds in a tubular feeder with correspondingly tiny ports, from which the finches extract one seed at a time.

Sunflower seed and wild bird seed mixtures can be placed either in tube feeders with larger ports, in wooden box feeders, or on feeding trays.

Four feeding niches. To attract the maximum numbers and varieties of birds to the backyard in winter, food should be offered in four feeding niches. Ground feeders such as sparrows and

On a typical winter day, the dozen or more bird feeders located at various levels on our patio are loaded with chickadees, nuthatches, juncos, tree sparrows, goldfinches, pine siskins, mourning doves, and downy woodpeckers.

doves seem most content with food sprinkled on the ground or on top of the snow. Cardinals, grosbeaks, and jays also will eat on the ground but prefer a level slightly above, which we call tabletop. If sunflower seeds or mixed seeds are placed on a tray or post feeder, preferably one with a roof to keep the food dry, that niche will be filled. Finches, chickadees, and titmice enjoy their food in hanging feeders. The more the feeder swings in the wind, the better these birds seem to like it. The fourth niche, which we call tree trunk, is where woodpeckers, brown creepers, and nuthatches feed on seed or beef suet.

Water:

North of the snow line, winter birds have an abundance of water in the form of snow. These birds are not in need of a

Even on a cold winter day, moving water has a certain magic for attracting birds.

drink and a bath as much as those species that spend their winters in the desert habitat of Arizona, for example. In the desert, great numbers of birds are more readily attracted to a water seep, waterhole, or pond than to food.

Yet even north of the snow line, water has a certain magic. Open water on a cold day, when temperatures are below freezing, will attract birds that ordinarily might not visit backyards.

On subfreezing days, bird pools can be kept ice-free with heaters, such as this one designed for livestock tanks.

A pool kept free of ice with an electric heater may offer the only open water in the area. And if the heated pool emits visible water vapor, it is all the more alluring.

Frost-free water. The challenge in providing water in winter for birds north of the snow line is to keep it from freezing. There are various water heaters on the market, but the most common are the submersible types. Large pools may be warmed with heaters made for livestock tanks. Another innovation, available in some bird feeder catalogs, is a birdbath that is simply heated by an electric light bulb.

Moving water is a magnet. Water that drips or splashes makes the best presentation. Birds are tuned in to water sounds and will be drawn from afar to the sound. The easiest way to make the water move is with a small water pump that moves about one hundred gallons of water an hour, like those manufactured by the Little Giant Pump Company, Oklahoma City, Oklahoma.

Each of the multitiered pools in our yard holds about fifty-five gallons of water. The three-tiered pool has a large reservoir in the bottom, a slightly smaller one on top, and a very small catch basin in between. The other pool has a large reservoir on the bottom, a small one on top and many rivulets of water in between, which flow over stones, shelves, and slides en route to the bottom.

Virtually all the species of winter birds that use our feeders also drink and bathe in the pools, and we occasionally see birds at the water that are not interested in feeding stations. They include golden-crowned kinglets, screech-owls, which drink at night in the illumination of patio spotlights, and flocks of cedar waxwings.

Appreciating the Birds of Prey

There are no guaranteed methods for attracting birds of prey to the backyard, and many people who feed birds would rather not have them threatening their beloved chickadees, goldfinches, and cardinals. Nevertheless, a backyard that extends an invitation in the form of an abundance of cover, food, and water to some birds is often attractive to hungry birds of prey as well.

We have, in fact, on rare occasions watched a kestrel, sharp-shinned hawk, or Cooper's hawk capture songbirds at our feeding station. Rather than being upset, we accept this natural behavior of magnificent raptors in action.

ATTRACTANTS FOR BIRDS OF WINTER

An abundance of cover in the form of mature trees (some with natural cavities or woodpecker holes), small trees, shrubs, and low-growing plants are essential for attracting the birds of winter. In addition, the following food, water, and shelter will enhance the attractiveness of your property to the winter species:

Hawks/Shrike—Songbirds at feeders will be the major attraction for hawks and northern shrikes. The greater the feeder activity, the greater the chances are that hawks and shrikes will come into the yard for a look, and possibly stay for dinner.

Water may also interest these birds. Kestrels might roost in vacant wood duck houses.

Owls—Though most owls are noctural, like hawks they may take an interest in the activity of smaller birds at the feeding stations. Some take mice from the ground under bird feeders. Screech-owls will readily use wood duck houses for roosting, and water might attract any number of owls in winter.

Gallinaceous Birds—All of the gallinaceous birds are seed eaters and may come to backyards in which they can feed on cracked corn and other grains. Providing lean-to shelters well supplied with grains will improve your chances of attracting the gallinaceous species in your area. Water will also attract them.

Woodpeckers—Beef suet, margarine, sunflower seeds, cracked corn, cracked walnuts and pecans, peanut butter, cheese, doughnuts, and corn bread may be of interest to woodpeckers. Present the food in baskets or wire feeders placed on tree trunks. They will drink water from ponds or pools. Vacant flicker houses might be attractive as roosting sites.

Corvids—Though they are omnivorous, most of the corvids relish seeds and nuts offered at bird feeders, particularly sunflower seeds and peanuts. Crows will be attracted to carrion. One woman actually collects a small road kill occasionally and deposits it in the far reaches of her backyard for crows and other scavengers.

Chickadees/Nuthatches/Creeper—Sunflower seeds (whole and hulled), cracked corn, cornmeal, doughnuts, peanut butter, chopped peanuts or nuts of any kind, beef suet, and water will lure these species. They will use almost any type of feeder.

Kinglets/Waxwings—Though these birds do not normally visit bird feeders, the waxwings are fond of the fruits and berries that grow on backyard trees and shrubs, including mountain ash, highbush cranberry, silky dogwood, autumn olive, crab apple, serviceberry, chokecherry, pyracantha, privet, and mulberry.

The Big Finches—Sunflower seeds, corn, oats, rice, millet, apples, corn bread, and wheat bread are eaten by this group. Offer the food on secured tray feeders or box feeders with plenty of standing room. They will bathe and drink from ponds and pools, and they also have a taste for salt.

The Little Finches—Sunflower seed (whole or hulled), niger seed, hemp seed, and red and white millet are ideal finch foods. Use hanging tube feeders or feeders on posts. They will bathe and drink at pools and ponds, and have been attracted to salt.

Juncos/Sparrows/Buntings—Cracked corn, red and white millet, and milo (sorghum) are favorites of these ground feeders. Spread food on the ground or on secured feeding trays or post feeders where there is ample standing room. They will drink and bathe at pools and ponds.

CHAPTER 14

Photographing the Birds of Winter

tanding knee-deep in snow, camera and tripod in hand, I waited for a flock of evening grosbeaks to return to the sunflower seeds on the big tray feeder thirty feet from me. I had been standing there for almost an hour on that 25°F day, and I was about to freeze.

Yet I was desperate for a photograph. As a Penn State journalism student at the time, I needed the photograph to illustrate an article on winter birds that I had written for *The Daily Collegian* student newspaper.

"Why don't you come inside and shoot your pictures through the window?" Dr. Hummer called from the back door of his dental clinic. "It's a lot more comfortable in here and the birds will return to the feeder much faster if you're inside and out of sight," he added.

By shooting through good quality window glass, you can produce excellent photographs of winter birds without going out into the cold.

What a great idea, I thought to myself. But Dr. Hummer was full of great ideas about his birds. He maintained the feeding station outside the window of his clinic to occupy the attention of his patients while he worked.

As soon as I moved inside, the grosbeaks returned to the feeder and I promptly shot all the photos I needed through Dr. Hummer's window glass.

Looking back on that day nearly thirty years ago, I realize that Dr. Hummer was responsible for opening a whole new world of photo opportunities for me. Since then, I have shot tens of thousands of photographs of birds through windows; some illustrate this book. A great many of them were photographed through the thermopane windows of our own living room. There is really no trick to it. We simply set up the camera on a tripod, place it as close to the window as possible, and use a telephoto lens to shoot photographs through the glass when the subjects and conditions are right.

On bright and sunny winter days, when the angle of the sun

is low and the color of the sunlight is rich, photographing birds through the window is a delight. I can afford to wait until every perch on the niger seed feeder is occupied by gold-finches, or until the male cardinal is positioned in exactly the right spot on the tray feeder, or until the red-bellied wood-pecker at the beef suet is facing the sun.

During the most active period of the winter bird-feeding season, I leave the camera set up on a tripod at the window for weeks, sometimes for more than a month at a time.

No Reflections

By placing the camera as close to the glass as possible and keeping the room behind you as dark as possible you can eliminate reflections. Shooting through quality glass results in no distortion in the pictures, even when the camera is positioned at a severe angle.

If a flash is required, reflections from it can be eliminated by positioning the flash unit or units against the glass.

Older windows are often ripply and not of a quality that will allow flawless photographs to be made through them. This was the case when we visited friends living in an old house in Pennsylvania. They had several pheasants coming regularly for the cracked corn in their backyard, and I wanted to photograph them. I was able to shoot as many photographs as I wanted of a particularly magnificent rooster by simply opening the window, setting the camera on a tripod, and focusing on the pheasant's feeding area. Aside from increasing our friends' heating bill a little that day, the system worked perfectly.

Cars Are Great Blinds, Too

Most of the advantages of photographing the birds of winter from inside a house apply to photographing them from inside a car. Birds usually have no fear of vehicles. Use your car as a blind at a winter birding hot spot (see Appendix), for example, or wherever winter birds can be approached in a vehicle. Auto-mobile glass is not as good to photograph through as the window glass in houses, but a car window can be lowered and photographs can be made easily through the open window.

A device that clamps onto the car door or window for holding a camera, much as a tripod does, will eliminate camera movement.

Shooting from inside a car saved both the camera equipment and this photographer from the misery of exceptionally cold weather recently on the banks of the Mississippi River. A flock of bald eagles spends much of each winter at a power plant just north of the town of Cassville, Wisconsin, where the plant's effluent warms the water around the plant and keeps it ice-free all winter. The eagles feed on the fish that are stunned or killed by the power plant's turbines.

The river water may have been warm but the ambient air certainly wasn't on the sunny January day we were there. But the subzero temperatures didn't seem to bother the eagles, which were perched in trees on the Iowa side of the river watching for fish. We waited several hours before the birds were close enough for photographs. Fortunately, we had the warm car in which to wait or we never would have persevered.

Cars also make first-rate blinds for bird photography.

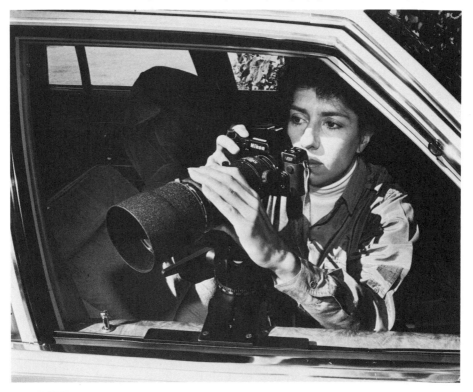

If you must go outside to photograph birds in extremely cold weather, you'll have to take some precautions, such as carrying spare film and batteries near your body to keep them warm.

Cold Weather Problems

Wintering flocks of bald eagles or a solitary snowy owl watching for prey from a fence post in a corn field are not likely to be found just outside the warm comfort of a living room. Sometimes they aren't accessible even from a car window. If the only way to get photographs of winter birds is to be out in the cold, then the photographic problems that the cold temperatures may create must be addressed. Unless some precautions are taken, cold weather can easily ruin the photo opportunities of a lifetime by adversely affecting camera equipment, film, and the efficiency of the photographer.

Subfreezing temperatures can cause batteries to lose power, slow the operation of spring-operated shutters, and blur viewfinders with frost formed by vapor condensation from the photographer's breath.

In extremely cold temperatures, the metal parts of the camera are dangerous to touch, as bare skin may stick to the metal. One bird photographer accidentally touched a metal part with his tongue and tragically left part of it on the camera.

Because modern cameras depend so heavily on batteries to operate virtually all of their systems—exposure meter, exposure setting, focusing, winding, rewinding, and flash—the power of those batteries is crucial to the proper operation of the cameras. In cold weather, batteries may not have enough strength to operate the systems correctly. Therefore, a photographer working for prolonged periods in cold weather should carry spare batteries in a pocket where the body will warm them.

Film will also freeze, lowering its sensitivity to light and color and causing incorrect exposures. It is not a good idea to store film in refrigerators or in cars that are parked overnight in extremely cold temperatures unless you allow the film to warm for a couple of hours at room temperature.

Condensation on camera viewfinders, lenses, and film caused by dramatic changes in temperature and humidity between inside and outside climates can also result in poor quality photographs. You can avoid condensation on your camera and film by following a recommendation from our friend Lefty Kreh, who suggests that before coming inside you slip your camera into a plastic bag, squeeze the air out of the bag, and then seal it. That will allow the camera to warm without condensation collecting on it.

Beware of snow falling on the lens. Unless removed, the droplets of moisture on the front of the lens will cause blurred spots in the photographs.

Photographers working in extremely cold locations, such as the polar regions or on mountain tops, can have their cameras "winterized" with special lubricants that will not freeze. But this isn't necessary for most modern cameras used in most kinds of winter weather.

Of course, all of these cold-weather problems can be avoided by simply photographing winter birds from inside a house or a vehicle where you and your camera equipment can stay warm and dry.

All Cameras Are Good

In this day of high-tech camera equipment, there are no bad cameras on the market. They are all capable of making excellent photographs. The difference in cost usually reflects the difference in durability and in options available. For example, cameras with telephoto lenses allow photographers to record larger images of the birds they photograph. Nevertheless, with a modern camera, even a point-and-shoot camera, you can make superb photographs of birds in winter, particularly if you catch the birds at feeders on the other side of your windows.

Bring the Birds in Close

The best way to take great photographs of winter birds in your backyard is to position bird feeders near enough to the windows so that you can see and photograph the birds at close range. As long as there is sufficient cover, such as trees, shrubs, or brush, birds will accept feeders situated close to windows. In fact, feeders that can be attached right to the glass with suction cups provide excellent opportunities for extreme close-ups of the birds that frequent them. For photographs of birds away from feeders but close to the window, try placing a tree branch next to the feeder, where the birds will land as they approach the food.

Even with basic camera equipment, impressive photographs of birds can be made if the feeders are located close to the windows.

When positioning bird feeders, birdbaths, and perches for optimum viewing and photography, keep these points in mind:

Background—If you place some kind of natural background, such as a shrub or evergreen tree, behind the feeder, the birds will show up better. For maximum color in the background, you could place a piece of colored cardboard or drape a colorful fabric behind the feeder. The important thing is to be certain that the background will display the bird, not distract attention from it.

Simple backgrounds show off both the birds and the feeders.

Lighting—The location of the sun in relation to the birds on the feeder is important. Ideally, the sun should shine on the subject so that it is well illuminated. The sun should not shine directly into the camera lens, but it should illuminate the subject adequately.

If the feeder is located so close to the window glass that the sun cannot shine on the birds using it, a flash may be required. Place the flash against the window or as close to it as possible to eliminate reflections.

When birds are photographed in snow scenes, the extreme brightness of the snow often deceives light meters, or cameras with automatic exposure meters, into making the birds in the photograph too dark. To correct this, override the meter or camera by opening the lens as much as two more *f* stops, to allow more light through the lens than is indicated. If an exposure override is not available on your camera, set the film speed lower (slower).

Composition—Before taking any photograph, look through the viewfinder at the composition. Is it best to place the subject in the center of the photograph? Or would it look better slightly off-center? Is the camera angle too high? Too low? Are you close enough? Too far away? Consider all of these points before pushing the button.

Photographs of birds away from feeders are easy to shoot if you place a twig just outside the window, but near a feeder.

Tripod—More photographs are ruined by camera movement than by any other cause. Whenever possible, place the camera on a tripod. If a fast shutter speed is not required to stop the movement of the subject, a tripod will also allow the use of slower film or slower shutter speed to give the photograph more sharpness (depth of field) from foreground to background.

Film—The film you select for photographing winter birds depends on how you want to use your pictures. If you plan to present slide shows for entertainment or education, or if you plan to publish your photographs, you should shoot slide film (color transparencies). On the other hand, if you want to keep a photo album of the birds, or send pictures to friends and relatives, or frame them for your wall, you should shoot print film.

Photographs of winter birds make attractive Christmas cards. Not only are they lovely and very appropriate for the season, but they are also personal creations which you can share with others.

Birds of Winter Hot Spots

The following are places in North America where the birds of winter can be seen, photographed, and generally enjoyed in their natural habitat. All of these facilities welcome bird watchers in winter:

NORTHEASTERN UNITED STATES

Maine

Acadia National Park, Box 177, Bar Harbor, ME 04609. (207) 288-3338. Features sea ducks, common ravens, red-breasted nuthatches, golden-crowned kinglets, purple finches, red crossbills, white-winged crossbills, and evening grosbeaks.

Petit Manan National Wildlife Refuge, Box 279, Milbridge, ME 04658. (207) 546-2124. Tours on request. Features sea ducks, spruce grouse, and boreal chickadees.

New Hampshire

White Mountain National Forest, Box 638, Laconia, NH 03247. (603) 528-8721. Features spruce grouse, three-toed woodpeckers, boreal chickadees, red crossbills, and white-winged crossbills.

New Jersey

Great Swamp National Wildlife Refuge, R.D. 1, Box 152, Basking Ridge, NJ 07920. (201) 647-1222. Two observation blinds with bird feeders located at each blind and another feeder at refuge headquarters. Features red-tailed hawks, American kestrels, barred owls, northern cardinals, white-throated sparrows, and house finches.

New York

Long Island National Wildlife Refuge Complex, Box 21, Shirley, NY 11967. (516) 286-0485. Self-guiding trails. Features northern bobwhites, black-capped chickadees, tufted titmice, and northern cardinals.

Pennsylvania

Allegheny National Forest, Box 847, Warren, PA 16365. (814) 723-5150. Features bald eagles.

Rhode Island

Sachuest Point National Wildlife Refuge, c/o Ninigret National Wildlife Refuge Complex, Box 307, Charlestown, RI 02813. (401) 364-9124. Observation platforms, guided bird walks, and visitor contact stations. Features sea ducks, rough-legged hawks, snowy owls, and short-eared owls.

MIDWESTERN UNITED STATES

Illinois

Chautauqua National Wildlife Refuge, R.R. 2, Box 61-B, Havana, IL 62644. (309) 535-2290. Features as many as fifty bald eagles.

Iowa

DeSoto National Wildlife Refuge, Route 1, Box 114, Missouri Valley, IA 51555. (712) 642-4121. Photo blind and viewing platform available by reservation for use in viewing migratory waterfowl in early December. Feeders at visitor center. Features some bald cagles, about 400,000 snow geese, northern bobwhites, mourning doves, and cedar waxwings.

Michigan

Huron-Manistee National Forest, 421 South Mitchell Street, Cadillac, MI 49601. (616) 775-2421. Features wild turkeys and horned larks.

Minnesota

Agassiz National Wildlife Refuge, R.R. 1, Box 74, Middle River, MN 56737. (218) 449-4115. Two bird feeders. Phone for snow conditions before going to the refuge. Features common ravens, northern shrikes, snow buntings, and common redpolls.

Rice Lake National Wildlife Refuge, Route 2, Box 67, McGregor, MN 55760. (218) 768-2402. Feeding station. Features rough-legged hawks, barred owls, sharp-tailed grouse, common ravens, evening grosbeaks, snow buntings, and common redpolls.

Superior National Forest, Box 338, Duluth, MN 55801. (218) 720-5481. Tours can be arranged. Features boreal owls, great gray owls, and snowy owls.

Tamarac National Wildlife Refuge, H.C. 10, Box 145, Rochert, MN 56578. (218) 847-2641. Visitor center. Feeding stations.

Appendix

Features pileated woodpeckers and large flocks of snow buntings.

North Dakota

Crosby Wetlands Management District, 206 North Main, Crosby, ND 58730. (701) 965-6488. Features gray partridge, ring-necked pheasants, sharp-tailed grouse, Bohemian waxwings, horned larks, Lapland longspurs, and snow buntings.

Sullys Hill National Game Preserve, U.S. Fish and Wildlife Service, Box 908, Devils Lake, ND 58301. (701) 766-4272. Blind available. Features snowy owls, gray partridge, horned larks, black-billed magpies, and snow buntings.

Wisconsin

Necedah National Wildlife Refuge, Star Route West, Box 386, Necedah, WI 54646. (608) 565-2551. Feeding stations near headquarters, auto tour, slide shows/guided tours upon request. Features bald eagles and wild turkeys.

WESTERN UNITED STATES

Colorado

Arapaho National Wildlife Refuge, Box 457, 953 Jackson County Road, #32, Walden, CO 80480. (303) 723-8202. Features golden eagles, sage grouse, and rosy finches.

Monte Vista National Wildlife Refuge, Box 1148, Alamosa, CO 81101. (719) 589-4021. Major wintering area for bald eagles, northern harriers, and rough-legged hawks.

Pawnee National Grassland, 660 "O" Street, Greeley, CO 80631. (303) 353-5004. Self-guided auto tour. Features golden eagles, rough-legged hawks, and American kestrels.

Rocky Mountain National Park, Estes Park, CO 80517. (303) 586-2371, ext. 225. Naturalist staff. Features golden eagles, blue grouse, white-tailed ptarmigans, three-toed woodpeckers, Clark's nutcrackers, mountain chickadees, pygmy nuthatches, red crossbills, evening and pine grosbeaks, and rosy finches.

San Juan National Forest, 701 Camino Del Rio, Durango, CO 81301. (303) 247-4874. Features wintering bald eagles along river areas and Lewis' woodpeckers.

Montana

Bowdoin National Wildlife Refuge, Box J, Malta, MT 59538. (406) 654-2863. Auto tour route. Feeders at refuge headquarters. Features bald eagles, northern goshawks, gyrfalcons, snowy owls, northern saw-whet owls, gray partridge, sharp-tailed grouse, northern shrikes, and Bohemian waxwings.

Charles M. Russell National Wildlife Refuge, Box 110, Lewistown, MT 59457. (406) 538-8706. Features bald eagles, rough-legged hawks, golden eagles, sage grouse, sharp-tailed grouse, horned larks, black-billed magpies, and Bohemian waxings.

Custer National Forest, Supervisor's Office, Box 2556, Billings, MT 59103. (406) 657-6361. Photo blinds, watchable wildlife points, and road tours. Features rough-legged hawks, gyrfalcons, and common redpolls.

Glacier National Park, West Glacier, MT 59936. (406) 888-5441. Features a concentration of bald eagles on lower McDonald Creek. Photo blinds are available.

Lee Metcalf National Wildlife Refuge, Box 257, Stevensville, MT 59870. (406) 777-5552. Features bald eagles, rough-legged hawks, and golden eagles.

Lolo National Forest, Building 24, Fort Missoula, Missoula, MT 59801. (406) 329-3750. Brochures and auto tours. Features bald eagles, red-tailed hawks, golden eagles, great horned owls, northern pygmy-owls, blue grouse, gray jays, Steller's jays, black-billed magpies, Bohemian waxwings, and Cassin's finches.

Warm Springs Wildlife Management Area, Warm Springs, MT 59756. (406) 693-7395. Features horned larks, gray jays, Steller's jays, Clark's nutcrackers, Bohemian waxwings, and snow buntings.

Oregon

Bear Valley Bald Eagle Refuge and Klamath Wildlife Area, Oregon Department of Fish and Wildlife, 1400 Miller Island Road West, Klamath Falls, OR 97603. (503) 883-5732. Bird lists and occasional guided tours (by appointment). Features wintering waterfowl and largest concentration of wintering bald eagles in the lower forty-eight states (300 to 500 annually).

Ochoco National Forest, Box 490, 155 North Court Street, Prineville, OR 97754. (503) 447-6247. Features wintering bald eagles.

Washington

Columbia National Wildlife Refuge, 735 East Main Street, Drawer F, Othello, WA 99344. (509) 488-2668. Features wintering waterfowl and bald eagles.

Nisqually National Wildlife Refuge, 100 Brown Farm Road, Olympia, WA 98506. (206) 753-9467. Two photo blinds and two observation decks/towers. Features wintering waterfowl and raptors.

Wyoming

Seedskadee National Wildlife Refuge, Box 700, Green River, WY 82935. (307) 875-2187. Primitive photo blinds. Features bald eagles, rough-legged hawks, golden eagles, sage grouse, boreal chickadees, and rosy finches.

Yellowstone National Park, National Park Service, Box 168, Yellowstone National Park, WY 82190. (307) 344-7381, ext. 2255. Features bald eagles, great gray owls, boreal owls, Clark's nutcrackers, mountain chickadees, northern shrikes, and Bohemian waxwings.

SOUTHEASTERN CANADA

New Brunswick

Fundy National Park, P.O. Box 40, Alma, New Brunswick EOA 1BO. (506) 887-2000. Features northern goshawks, black-backed woodpeckers, gray jays, boreal chickadees, and white-winged crossbills.

Prince Edward Island
Prince Edward Island National Park, P.O. Box 487, Charlottetown, P.E.I. C1A 7L1. (902) 672-2211. Guided tours upon request. Features snowy owls, evening grosbeaks, Lapland longspurs, and snow buntings.

Quebec
Forillon National Park, C.P. 1220, Gaspé, Quebec GOC 1RO. (418) 892-5553. Features boreal chickadees, red-breasted nuthatches, northern shrikes, pine grosbeaks, red crossbills, white-winged crossbills, evening grosbeaks, and common redpolls.

SOUTH CENTRAL CANADA

Saskatchewan
Prince Albert National Park, Box 100, Waskesiu, Saskatchewan SOJ 2YO. (306) 663-5322. Features great gray owls, boreal owls, pileated woodpeckers, and three-toed woodpeckers.

SOUTHWESTERN CANADA

British Columbia
Kootenay National Park, Box 220, Radium Hot Springs, British Columbia VOA 1MO. (604) 347-9615. Features northern hawk owls.

Mount Revelstoke/Glacier National Parks, P.O. Box 350, Revelstoke, British Columbia VOE 2SO. (604) 837-5155. Features northern pygmy-owls, spruce grouse, blue grouse, white-tailed ptarmigans, three-toed woodpeckers, pileated woodpeckers, gray jays, Steller's jays, Clark's nutcrackers, and mountain chickadees.

PHOTO CREDITS

All photographs are by the authors, except those noted below.

Ron Austing, pages 9, 15, 21, 22, 25, 36, 39, 42, 43, 52, 59 (bottom), 66, 68, 75, 95, 103, 109 (bottom), 119, 128 (bottom), 133, 134, 139

P. G. Connors/Vireo, page 128 (top)

Thomas C. Grubb, Jr., page 67

Hal H. Harrison, pages 79, 91, 97

S. LaFrance/Vireo, page 137

Duane G. Manthei, page 87

Karl and Stephen Maslowski, pages 85, 129

Steve Maslowski, page 84

Maslowski Wildlife Productions, pages 16, 32, 50, 74, 80, 81, 99, 101, 109 (top), 146

R. Mellon/Vireo, page 62

Ray Quigley, pages 78, 122
Len Rue, Jr., page 47
Leonard Rue Enterprises, pages 54, 55, 56, 60, 121
John L. Tveten, page 123
Gary R. Zahm, page 57

BIBLIOGRAPHY

Ambrose, Dave. 1984. "Savage Winter." *Outdoor Highlights,* Vol. 12, No. 3, pp. 3–7. Illinois Department of Conservation, Springfield.

Audubon, John James. 1842. *The Birds of America,* Vol. 4. New York: Geo. R. Lockwood and Son.

Beal, Foster E. L. 1897. *Some Common Birds in Their Relation to Agriculture.* U.S. Department of Agriculture Farmers' Bulletin 54. Washington, D.C.: U.S. Government Printing Office.

Bendell, J. F. 1973. *Ruffed Grouse.* Information Canada, Ottawa.

Bent, Arthur Cleveland. 1968. *Life Histories of North American Cardinals, Grosbeaks, Buntings, Towhees, Finches, Sparrows and Allies.* Smithsonian Institution United States National Museum *Bulletin 237.* Parts One, Two and Three. Compiled and edited by Oliver L. Austin, Jr. Smithsonian Institution Press, Washington, D.C.

————. 1963. *Life Histories of North American Flycatchers, Larks, Swallows and Their Allies.* Dover Publications, Inc., New York. (Originally published as Smithsonian Institution United States National Museum *Bulletin 179.* United States Government Printing Office. 1942.)

————. 1963. *Life Histories of North American Gallinaceous Birds.* Dover Publications, Inc., New York. (Originally published as Smithsonian Institution United States National Museum *Bulletin 162.* United States Government Printing Office. 1932.)

————. 1964. *Life Histories of North American Jays, Crows and Titmice.* Parts One and Two. Dover Publications, Inc., New York. (Originally published as Smithsonian Institution United States National Museum *Bulletin 191.* United States Government Printing Office. 1946.)

————. 1964. *Life Histories of North American Nuthatches, Wrens, Thrashers, and Their Allies.* Dover Publications, Inc., New York. (Originally published as Smithsonian Institution United States National Museum *Bulletin 195.* United States Government Printing Office. 1948.)

————. 1964. *Life Histories of North American Thrushes, Kinglets, and Their Allies.* Dover Publications, Inc., New York. (Originally published as Smithsonian Institution United States National Museum *Bulletin 196.* United States Government Printing Office. 1949.)

————. 1965. *Life Histories of North American Wagtails, Shrikes, Vireos, and Their Allies.* Dover Publications, Inc., New York. (Originally published as Smithsonian Institution United States National Museum *Bulletin 197.* United States Government Printing Office, 1950.)

————. 1964. *Life Histories of North American Woodpeckers.* Dover Publications, New York. (Originally published as Smithsonian Institution United States National Museum *Bulletin 174.* United States Government Printing Office. 1939.)

Bonney, Richard E., Jr. 1983. "More Than Just a Pretty Face." *The Living Bird Quarterly,* Winter, pp. 11–13.

Brittingham, Margaret Clark, and Stanley A. Temple. 1986. "A Survey of Avian Mortality at Winter Feeders." *Wildlife Society Bulletin,* Vol. 14, No. 4, pp. 445–450.

Brody, Jane E. 1987. "Cold-Weather Survival Tactics Revealed in New Studies." *The New York Times,* December 15.

Burnell, Kristi L., and Diana F. Tomback. 1985. "Steller's Jays Steal Gray Jay Caches: Field and Laboratory Observations." *Auk,* Vol. 102, No. 2, pp. 417–418.

Cahalane, Victor H. 1944. "A Nutcracker's Search for Buried Food." *Auk,* Vol. 61, p. 643.

Canadian Wildlife Service. 1973. *Ring-necked Pheasant.* Catalog No. CW69-4/33. Information Canada, Ottawa.

Clapp, Roger B. 1976. "Review of Longevity Records by W. Rydzewski." *Bird Banding,* Vol. 47, No. 3, pp. 279–281.

Clapp, Roger B., M. Kathleen Klimkiewicz, and Anthony G. Futcher. 1983. "Longevity Records of North American Birds: *Columbidae* through *Paridae.*" *Journal of Field Ornithology,* Vol. 54, No. 2, pp. 128–130.

Colvin, Bruce A., and Steven R. Spaulding. 1983. "Winter Foraging Behavior of Short-eared Owls *(Asio flammeus)* in Ohio." *The American Midland Naturalist,* July, pp. 124–128.

Cornell Laboratory of Ornithology. 1978. "Winter Finches." *Newsletter to Members,* Winter, pp. 6–7.

Coues, Elliott. 1874. *Birds of the Northwest: A Handbook of Ornithology.* Washington, D.C.: U.S. Government Printing Office.

Cushman, Ruth Carol. 1980. "On the Ptrail of the Ptarmigan." *American Forests,* December, pp. 46–49.

Dunn, Erica H. 1989. "FeederWatch 1988–89: Mid-Year Results." *FeederWatch News,* Vol. 2, No. 1, pp. 1–2. Cornell Laboratory of Ornithology, Ithaca, New York.

————. 1989. "1988–89 Annual Report." *FeederWatch News,* Vol. 2, No. 2, pp. 1–4. Cornell Laboratory of Ornithology, Ithaca, New York.

————. 1989. "Winter's Wanderers: Boom and Bust in Pine Siskin." *FeederWatch News,* Vol. 2, No. 2, pp. 5–7. Cornell Laboratory of Ornithology, Ithaca, New York.

Ehrlich, Paul R., David S. Dobkin and Darryl Wheye. 1988. *The Birder's Handbook.* New York: Simon and Schuster/Fireside Books.

Farrand, John, Jr., ed. 1983. *The Audubon Society Master Guide to Birding.* 3 volumes. New York: Alfred A. Knopf.

Forbush, Edward H. 1907. *Useful Birds and Their Protection.* Boston: Massachusetts State Board of Agriculture.

Fowler, Ron, Carl Trautman, et al. 1975. *The Pheasant in South Dakota.* South Dakota Department of Game, Fish and Parks, Pierre.

George, Jean. 1967. "Long Night of the Snowbirds." *National Wildlife,* December, pp. 14–17.

George, William G., and Robert Sulski. 1984. "Thawing of Frozen Prey by a Great Horned Owl." *Canadian Journal of Zoology,* February, pp. 314–315.

Grooms, Steve. 1984. "The Survivors." *Fins and Feathers,* December, pp. 26–29.

Harrison, George H. 1979. *The Backyard Bird Watcher.* New York: Simon & Schuster.

Harrison, Hal H. 1948. *American Birds in Color.* New York: Wm. H. Wise & Co., Inc.

Harrison, Kit and George. 1985. *America's Favorite Backyard Birds.* New York: Simon & Schuster.

Kennard, J. H. 1975. "Longevity Records of North American Birds." *Bird-Banding,* Vol. 46, No. 1, pp. 55–73.

Kerth, T. R. 1986. "Just a Crow." *Outdoor Highlights,* Vol. 14, No. 9, pp. 10–12. Illinois Department of Conservation, Springfield.

Kilpatrick, H. J., T. P. Husband, and C. A. Pringle. 1988. "Winter Roost Site Characteristics of Eastern Wild Turkeys." *Journal of Wildlife Management,* Vol. 52, No. 3, pp. 461–463.

Kreh, Lefty, 1988. *The L. L. Bean Guide to Outdoor Photography.* New York: Random House.

Lawrence, Louise de Kiriline. 1973. *Gray Jay.* Catalog No. CW 69-4/29. Information Canada, Ottawa.

Lemmon, Robert S. 1951. *Our Amazing Birds.* Garden City, New York: Doubleday & Company, Inc.

Mundinger, Paul C. and Sylvia Hope. 1982. "Expansion of the Winter Range of the House Finch: 1947–79." *American Birds,* July, Vol. 36, No. 4.

Nero, Robert W. 1973. *Blue Jay.* Catalog No. CW69-4/22. Information Canada, Ottawa.

————. 1988. "Denizen of the Northern Forests." *Birder's World,* September/October, pp. 20–25.

————. 1973. *Red-Breasted Nuthatch.* Information Canada, Ottawa.

Parks, G. Hapgood. 1973. *Evening Grosbeak.* Information Canada, Ottawa.

Peterson, Roger Tory. 1947. *A Field Guide to the Birds.* Boston: Houghton Mifflin Company.

Robbins, Chandler S., Bertel Bruun, and Herbert S. Zim. 1986. *A Guide to Field Identification—Birds of North America.* New York: Golden Press.

Sayre, Roxanna. 1980. "An Invasion to Remember." *Audubon,* January, p. 52.

Scott, Shirley L., ed. 1983. *Field Guide to the Birds of North America.* Washington, D.C.: National Geographic Society.

Smith, Charles. R. 1979. "Chickadees in Winter." *Newsletter to*

Members, Winter. Cornell Laboratory of Ornithology, Ithaca, New York.

Smith, Dwight G., Arnold Devine, and Ray Gilbert. 1987. "Screech Owl Roost Site Selection." *Birding,* August, pp. 6–15.

Smith, Ned. 1965. "King of the Winter Woods." *Pennsylvania Game News,* February, pp. 3–6.

————. 1965. "The Wanderers." *Pennsylvania Game News,* December.

Steinbacher, J. 1964. "Woodpecker." *A New Dictionary of Birds,* ed. A. L. Thompson. New York: McGraw-Hill Book Company.

Stokes, Donald and Lillian. 1983. "The Virtues of 'It'—and Juncos!" *Bird Watcher's Digest,* November/December, pp. 75–77.

Swengel, Ann B. 1987. "The Habits of the Northern Saw-Whet Owl." *Passenger Pigeon,* Fall, pp. 127–133.

Terres, John K. 1980. *The Audubon Society Encyclopedia of North American Birds.* New York: Alfred A. Knopf.

Torrey, Bradford. 1885. *Birds in the Bush.* Boston: Houghton Mifflin Company.

Townsend, Charles W. 1905. "The Birds of Essex County, Mass." *Mem. Nuttall Ornithological Club,* No. 3. Cambridge, Mass.

Vander Haegen, W. M., M. W. Sayre, and W. E. Dodge. 1989. "Winter Use of Agricultural Habitats by Wild Turkeys in Massachusetts." *Journal of Wildlife Management,* Vol. 53, No. 1, pp. 30–33.

Weeden, R. B. 1974. *Ptarmigans.* Canadian Wildlife Service. Information Canada, Ottawa.

Wernert, Susan, J., ed. 1982. *North American Wildlife.* Pleasantville, New York: Reader's Digest.

Wise, Sherry. 1986. *The Ring-necked Pheasant.* Wisconsin Department of Natural Resources, Bureau of Wildlife Management, Madison.

————. 1986. *The Sharp-Tailed Grouse.* Wisconsin Department of Natural Resources, Bureau of Wildlife Management, Madison.

Wise, Sherry, and John Kubisiak. 1986. *The Ruffed Grouse.* Wisconsin Department of Natural Resources, Bureau of Wildlife Management, Madison.

Woodcock, John. 1913. "A Friendly Chickadee." *Bird Lore,* Vol. 15, pp. 373–75.

Yannone, Vince. 1982. "Waxwings." *Montana Outdoors,* January 11. Montana Department of Fish, Wildlife and Parks, Helena, Montana.

INDEX

Page numbers in *italics* refer to illustrations.

About the Authors

KIT and GEORGE HARRISON are writers, photographers, book authors, and consultants in the field of natural history and the outdoors. They have traveled throughout the world in search of nature adventures on assignments for national magazines, but they specialize in the birds of the backyard.

When not studying or photographing the birds in their own backyard in southeastern Wisconsin, Kit works as the conservation editor of *Sports Afield* magazine. George is the nature editor of *Sports Afield* magazine and field editor for *National Wildlife* and *International Wildlife* magazines.

Other bird books the Harrisons have written include *Roger Tory Peterson's Dozen Birding Hot Spots* (Simon & Schuster, 1976), *The Backyard Bird Watcher* (Simon & Schuster, 1979), *America's Favorite Backyard Birds* (Simon & Schuster, 1983), *A Beginner's Guide to Bird Watching* (National Audubon Society, 1986), and *George Harrison's Birdwatching Diary* (Diaries, Inc., 1989).